JOURNEYS T
BRIGANTIA

JOHN DIXON
AND
PHILLIP DIXON

VOLUME EIGHT:

Circular Walks in
The Forest of Bowland

JOURNEYS THROUGH BRIGANTIA

VOLUME EIGHT:

CIRCULAR WALKS IN
THE FOREST OF BOWLAND

By

John Dixon & Phillip Dixon

Copyright © John Dixon & Phillip Dixon 1992
ALL RIGHTS RESERVED

Published by Aussteiger Publications,
8 Back Skipton Road, Barnoldswick BB8 5NE.
Tel. (0282) 812741

Typeset by:
Hargreaves Steel Limited,
133 Henry Street, Church, Accrington, Lancashire BB5 4EP

Printed by:
Lamberts of Settle

First edition, July 1992
Second Edition, June 1993
ISBN 1 872764 04 5

The sketch maps in this book are intended to indicate the route in a general way.
Walkers should use Ordnance Survey Pathfinder maps to locate exact routes.

Whilst all the walks use established and definitive footpaths (unless otherwise stated in
the text), walkers are requested to respect the privacy of residents and not to stray from
the footpaths.
If you find that a footpath has been obstructed, please report the matter on your return
to: The County Surveyor, M. F. Callery, P.O. Box 9, Guild House, Preston PR1 8RD.

PLEASE OBSERVE THE COUNTRY CODE.

Dedicated to my old friend John Mitchell. In the early 1960s we wandered far and wide
throughout Bowland exploring every hill and glade — wonderful days.
Good health, Mitch — John

AUSSTEIGER PUBLICATIONS

Contents

AUSSTEIGER HISTORICAL FIELD GUIDES

Historic Walks around the Pendle Way   1990

JOURNEYS THROUGH BRIGANTIA

VOLUME ONE: 1990
Craven, Airedale & Wharfedale

VOLUME TWO: 1990
Ribblesdale, Malham & Central Wharfedale

VOLUME THREE:
Lower Wharfedale, Washburndale & Ilkley Moor

VOLUME FOUR: 1991
'Beyond the Hill of Winds': Upper Ribblesdale,
The Three Peaks & Upper Wharfedale

VOLUME FIVE:
Nidderdale, Knaresborough & Wensleydale

VOLUME SIX:
Swaledale, Teesdale & the Vale of Eden

VOLUME SEVEN:
The Lune Valley & The Howgill Fells

VOLUME EIGHT: 1992 & 1993
The Forest of Bowland

VOLUME NINE: 1993
The Ribble Valley

VOLUME TEN:
Pendle & The Brönte South Pennines

VOLUME ELEVEN: 1993
The East Lancashire Pennines

Distributors:
Lancashire Books, 213 Chorley Old Road, Whittle-le-Woods, Chorley, PR6 7NP   0257 278613
Alan R. Hemsworth, Crow Trees Cottage, 10 Chapel Street, Settle, BD24 9HS   0729 822761

INTRODUCTION

These explorations take us through the finest upland landscape that Lancashire has to offer — the Forest of Bowland — an Area of Outstanding Natural Beauty. The Hodder Valley, the Vale of the Loud, the Langden Valley and the Trough of Bowland provide natural entry to the wild highlands of the fells — a peat and heather moorland with wind-torn gritstones gaping through. These remote tops provide a vital breeding ground for many species of birdlife: Curlews, Golden Plover, the Hen-Harrier, Ring Ouzel, Red Grouse and the Short Eared Owl find their food source and nesting sites here. The Merlin and the Peregrine Falcon are also visitors.

Down in the valleys the land is lush and green and much ancient woodland still exists. Hedges of blackthorn, hawthorn, holly and crab apple replace the drystone walls of the higher ground and provide an environment for all types of flora and small mammals.

The scattered villages and hamlets are quiet and unspoilt — a rustic arcadia steeped in history that reflects a time of Lancashire past.

The many farmsteads, that form the backbone and provide the lifeblood of the region's economy, possess a great wealth of historical and architectural heritage reflecting settlement patterns that go back to the Middle Ages and beyond.

The range and scope of this volume take in all my previous works, that are here extensively revised, and new source material and areas to explore not covered in any other work.

The walking is first class in this district so far undiscovered by the crowds who litter the "honeypots" of the Lakes and Dales. So get your boots on and make the most of what the Forest of Bowland has to offer.

Included in this Volume are many fine line drawings by the late Finnish artist Jaana Järvinen who worked with me on our previous Bowland books.

— John Dixon, Barnoldswick, 1992.

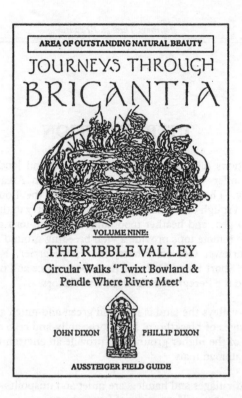

AREA OF OUTSTANDING NATURAL BEAUTY

JOURNEYS THROUGH
BRIGANTIA

VOLUME NINE:

THE RIBBLE VALLEY

Circular Walks "Twixt Bowland &
Pendle Where Rivers Meet'

JOHN DIXON   PHILLIP DIXON

AUSSTEIGER FIELD GUIDE

HISTORICAL BACKGROUND

IN 1963 our family moved into a bungalow on a small housing development situated on the southern slope of the lower Ribble Valley. The estate had little to recommend it in terms of architectural merit — being a good example of 1960s shoddy workmanship.

The abiding memory of those years can be divided into three areas — the seemingly endless wet winters, the boredom of school attendance and the magnificent panorama of the southern Bowland Fells viewed from our lounge window.

The main feature of the latter was the deep fold in the fells where the Hodder cuts between Longridge Fell — the most southerly named fell in Britain — and the fells around Browsholme.

On a clear day the summit of Ingleborough could be discerned to the north east. On such days it was possible to see, in the gap between Kemple End and Whitewell, a vista which took the eye deep into the heart of Bowland. Here was a landscape of eternal beauty largely untouched by the hand of industry.

On those long summer Sundays in the early 60s we would wander down to the riverbank at Hacking Hall — there was little else to do in those days. A walk to Hacking would continue to Dinkley suspension bridge, passing ancient burial mounds and farmsteads of a former age on the way.

On we would go via the virgin railway embankments of the abandoned Longridge to Gisburn railway to Stonyhurst, and on up through the old deer park to the summit of Longridge Fell. From this point we took in with our eyes the greater massif of the Bowland Fells — so near yet so far away.

We would then return home by way of Gallows Lane and Ribchester Bridge to wander on through the fields to Old Langho and on to 'the village of the folk of Billa'. Little did we know that these walks were tentatively preparing the field work on which our books are now based.

Just beyond the range of our Sunday walks lay Bowland proper. In a strict historical sense probably the Ribble was the southern and eastern edge of Bowland Forest in very ancient times. Today most accept that the watershed on the Waddington Fells between the Hodder and the Ribble and the northern escarpment of Longridge Fell mark the southern boundary of Bowland. The northern boundary has always been accepted as the Lunesdale watershed. The western boundary is the rampart of fells rising from the plain of Amounderness known as the Fylde.

Within these bounds lies the valley of the Hodder and its tributaries, this is the heart of Bowland. This fell-land area is of millstone grit on a sandstone underbed with outcrops of carboniferous limestone exposed mainly on the southern fells.

The great Craven and Dent faults separate Bowland from the western dales of Yorkshire, while the Ribble axis fault divides the forest from the coal seams of the Calder basin. The Ribble rises north east of Bowland and flows south to Gisburn.

The Craven drumlins blocked the post-Ice Age Ribble from flowing into the Aire, so the river turns south west to the sea at Preston. Within this massive crescent or bend lie the fells of Bowland. It would seem that the Anglo-Saxon place-name Bowland means 'the land in the bend'.

During the time we lived with our parents at Billington, a drive through Bowland was one of the highlights of a family weekend. From Whalley, with its three thousand years of settlement, we would take the back road to Lancaster via the Trough of Bowland.

We left Lancashire crossing the Ribble at Mitton where the marble effigies of the Shireburns slept in silent witness to the faith which rejected the ridiculous religious pretentions of the English throne. Passing shortly into Bashall we recalled references in ancient works to the mass graves in this parish — the result of a conflict lost to the mists of time. Behind a belt of trees stood the stately mansion of Browsholme, home of the Parkers who in olden times were hereditary keepers of the forest chase.

On the fell above the forest chapel of Whitewell we might stop to explore the old lime kiln and quarry. The fossils we picked up reminded one of how fleeting man's hold on the planet has been.

At a very early age I considered the Hodder Valley from Whitewell onwards to be one of the most outstanding landscapes that one could wish to behold. Little did we know then of the terrible events that took place hereabouts — where a single farmstead now represents a village extinguished by the brutal knights of William of Normandy. William's cruel descendants, who occupied by right of the sword alone the English crown, held these lands in the bondage of forest law until recent times.

At Dunsop we would leave the Hodder Valley and climb to the summit of the pass known as the Trough of Bowland. This side valley supports but three farms and in economic terms has developed very little in a thousand years. Here the scars on the fells tell of a long vanished industry that exploited the narrow veins of lead-bearing ore that are trapped in the limestone beds between here and Whitendale.

Beyond the Trough we return to Lancashire and the headwaters of the Wyre. The road sign to Abbeystead recalls an abortive settlement of Cistercian monks. Other signs in those days warned walkers off the fells with dire legal action.

A stop at Wyresdale prospect tower was compulsory. Here the great expanse of Morecambe Bay lay before us — the Sea of Rheged in Celtic times. Beyond the sands lay the fells of Cumbria, while on the coastal plain Blackpool's garish tower could be made out. On a clear evening a cloud on the north western horizon might have been the distant shore of Man.

It was from Man that the last Norse king came this way en route to pay homage at the court of Henry III. Harald of Man landed in Furness and with horses provided by the Abbot of Furness Abbey and a guide provided by the Prior of Cartmel would have crossed the Kent sands to the king's castle at Lancaster.

Next day guides would lead Harald's party up into the hills of Bowland, a thirty mile journey partly on foot to Sawley Abbey in Ribblesdale. From Sawley it was two or three days journey to the Bishop's palace at York. After which it was on to London. Having paid homage at Westminster, Harald would have returned to Furness via the Trough of Bowland. On this, his last homecoming, did he see the distant shore of Man from the heights of Wyresdale?

Because of the large proportion of high peat-laden moors in Bowland, settlement has been limited to a chain of hamlets in the main Hodder Valley and isolated farmsteads. Like Harald we tend to travel *through* Bowland rather than *to* Bowland. Bowland is a sparsely populated wilderness surrounded by more populated plains and valleys.

The great Iron Age trade route across the north of England passed to the south of Bowland. The Romans built a military road across the heart of Bowland linking Ribchester and their forts along the Lune Valley. Except for a watering post near Slaidburn there is no evidence of Roman settlement within the area.

The Celts of post-Roman Britain merged with the Anglian settlers from the east, and after the coming of the Norse in the tenth century we can be fairly certain that Bowland was as fully settled as at any time in history. During these days little used tracks would have linked the hamlets of Bowland.

The uprising against the Norman yoke in 1069 resulted in the depopulation of Bowland brought about by genocide. The moorland area between the Lune and the Ribble was subjected to forest law and maintained as a reserve for the king's court on their occasional hunting forays in the north of England.

During the Early Middle Ages the main trade routes through Bowland became established. The main Trough route brought the monastic wool packs from Furness, Man, Ireland and Galloway via Lancaster onwards into Yorkshire for transportation to Flanders and Tuscany.

A complex web of green roads linked the hamlets, monastic granges and farmsteads of Bowland. The products which the forest exported were wool, stock and other agricultural goods. The main requirements of Bowland were grain and salt.

From the salt fields of Cheshire, a series of routes brought the life-giving mineral to all parts of the Kingdom. On ponyback 100lb loads of hard salt would be carried across the Cheshire plain deep into the Pennines. The Hornby Road above Slaidburn is also known as Saltergate — 'the road of the salt merchants'. These long distance high fell routes offered free grazing en route for the pack-trains carrying wool or salt, lime or coal.

The great cattle drives of the mediaeval period kept to lowland routes, such as the Galloway Road which followed the route of the old A6 from north to south Lancashire. Place-names such as Galgate and Scotforth near Lancaster and Scotch Corner in Yorkshire recall these great mediaeval cattle drives from Scotland.

The Settlement of Bowland

The early history of Bowland has been ignored by most writers until recently. Having studied Bowland for a decade, the authors now feel that a broad pattern of settlement development can be defined with confidence. We do not claim all our findings to be original — full credit must be given to Chadwick, Jones and Smith.

We have taken the insights of academic research, personal field study and analysis and here present our findings to the reader. We do not deny that we are critics of the orthodox — excluded by self choice from the constraints of academic conventions. The history of Bowland, its fells and dales are a common heritage to be explored by us all.

The first evidence of human activity in Bowland comes from urn burials and habitation sites that date back to some time before 1800 BC — Fairy Holes Caves and the Bleasdale Circle site being good examples.

The barrows at Easington and Slaidburn and the great enclosure above Dinkling Green point to a fair amount of activity if not intensive settlement during the Bronze Age.

There is little evidence of Iron Age settlement within the area. Perhaps Iron Age farmers preferred the rich soils of Craven and the Fylde or the advantages of settlement in the Lune and Ribble Valleys rather than try to establish settlements in what was then a great oak forest.

The coming of Rome resulted in a great road being driven through the wilderness. A small watering post might have been established on the fell above Newton to serve this road. The Imperial authorities do not seem to have exploited the lead and silver ores of Bowland, but a massive industrial site at Quernmore provided roof tiles for the western and northern forts of Britain.

The collapse of Roman power in the fifth century saw the emergence of Celtic kingdoms in the north of England. Just south of Bowland a religious/political centre existed at Whalley. We believe that Bowland was an integral part of the Celtic kingdom of Rheged, dependent on the regional caput at Whalley.

This political dependency being reflected by the fact that all Forest areas of Bowland were dependent on the white Church of the Virgin and All Saints at Whalley — itself mother church of Blackburnshire.

The place-names of Bowland reflect the chronological pattern of settlement. The oldest settlements have Anglian place-names — Slaidburn, Newton, Burholme, Easington, Hammerton and Whitewell. These early settlements in the wilderness tended to be on land away from the wet valley floor, but below the high fells close to a suitable washing brook.

A settlement like the deserted hamlet of Burholme consisted of a forest chapel and a handful of rude huts. These hamlets were not units in their own right (manors) but merely out-settlements of the great manor of Grindleton in Ribblesdale.

The land-hungry Norse who fell upon the Irish Sea coast in the tenth century came as refugees from Dublin, Man and the Sodors (Western Isles). Many settled close by the sea on the marginal lands of the Fylde, West Derby and the Wirral. Some family groups pressed inland searching for vacant land. Deep in the high fells Viking farmsteads were established at Brennand, Whitendale and Gamble Hole, to name but a few.

The Normans depopulated Bowland and Amounderness. The main villages of the Fylde and Ribblesdale were repopulated within a few generations. The enforcement of Forest laws discouraged the resettlement of the Hodder Valley. Another factor which held back resettlement were the massive land grants to monastic houses in the 12th and 13th centuries. Kirkstall's sheep farms are to be found all around the upper Hodder Valley.

The brutal suppression of the monastic houses in the 16th century resulted in the full economic development of Bowland. The Stewart Kings licensed the mining of silver and lead ores and the last attempt to protect game is represented by the establishment of deer parks.

The break-up of the monastic granges into smaller holdings, allied to the shortage of wood for construction resulted in Bowland's rich heritage of 17th century yeoman houses. The close of the 17th century saw the final enclosure of the forest into private holdings.

The next two hundred years saw land ownership become more and more consolidated. Today, the great landowners of Bowland are the Crown, the Duke of Westminster and the regional water company.

In the 19th century, no railways were driven into Bowland. The lead mines became exhausted and there was no coal to exploit. The few textile mills established around the edge of Bowland tended to be small and transient. The dawn of this century found Bowland unspoilt by the industrial revolution.

The danger to the scenic beauty of Bowland was recognised when it was designated as an Area of Outstanding Natural Beauty in 1964. The Bowland Fells are the largest area of continuous heatherlands in Lancashire providing important breeding grounds for many upland and sea birds.

Water extraction and pine afforestation have been identified as potential dangers to the landscape of Bowland. However the authors are more concerned by the inflow of affluent settlers who work in the Lancashire conurbations. Should every farm and barn in Bowland be converted into a 'desirable' executive home?

Certain fields of study in Bowland have been looked at in a comprehensive manner — such as the lead trade and the encroachment of the forest in mediaeval times.

Bowland in the Iron Age, Roman and sub-Roman periods are still vague areas of study. The authors hope to present new papers on the early history of the church in Bowland and Iron Age field works in the next few years. Between our wide ranging field studies and comparative methods — down to the public funded key-hole archaeological methods at play in the area, there is still plenty of room for new research areas to be exploited.

History is, however, not the main reason why you should explore Bowland. Unlike the Lakes, these hills have not been made popular by the media. Bowland, though lacking the violent geology of the Lakes, has its own passive beauty. A beauty which can also have a deep economic/political significance.

If we compare these lands between the Lune and the Ribble with those twixt the Ribble and Mersey we may ask, "Was the false prosperity of the Industrial Revolution worth what our forefathers did in the valleys of the Roch, Irwell, Darwen and Calder?" Bowland is a silent witness to a landscape murdered for short-term economic greed.

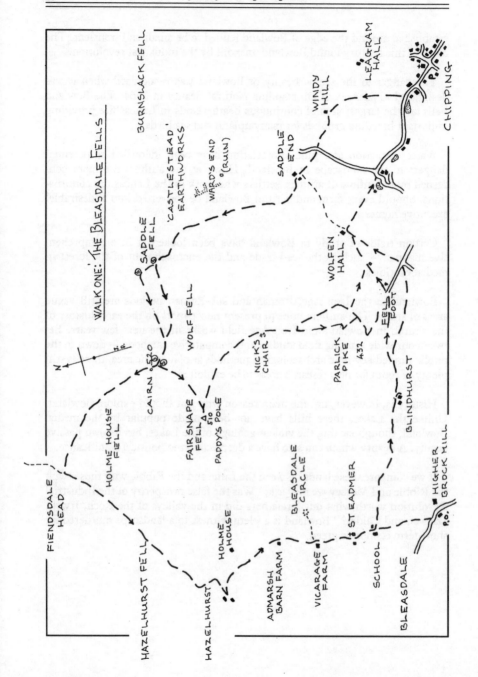

WALK ONE: THE BLEASDALE FELLS

WALK 1

THE BLEASDALE FELLS

13½ or 8 miles, 6 or 4 hours.

MAP: *O.S. SD 44/54 & SD 64/74 PATHFINDER*

LUNCH: *Bleasdale Post Office Cafe*

START: *Chipping Car Park*

Saddle Fell, Wolf Fell, Fair Snape Fell, Parlick Pike and Holme Head Fell are the south-west Bowland hills that make up the Bleasdale Fells. The longer walk takes in all these peaks in the form of a double horse-shoe with a return through the grassy meadows of the Bleasdale Amphitheatre to view that most ancient of Lancashire's monuments — the Bleasdale Circle.

The shorter walk takes in the major high points with a return over Parlick by way of Wolfen Hall. Two good walks in this spectacular corner of Bowland offering fine views over the County.

Chipping

The ancient fell-side market town of Chipping has origins that go back beyond recorded history. In c.1770, during road and building work to the north of the church, a Bronze Age burial mound was uncovered. An urn was revealed, marked with a lozenge decoration and containing fragments of bone.

Chipping acquired its status as a market centre during the Roman period. Wheat, being one of the primary staples of the Roman Army, was first cultivated in the newly cleared Vale of the Loud. This brought an age of prosperity to the district and a trading centre was soon established — horses, salt, lime, wheat and other grains being the major commodities exchanged. With the demise of Roman influence, the fields fell into decay and only moss-land and the place-name, 'Wheatley', attest to Chipping's former 'Golden Wealth'.

Both the Sun Inn and the Talbot Arms provide good watering holes for the traveller passing through this high valley, and I recommend both to you.

Today the village is associated with the manufacture of chairs. This enterprise started in the mid 19th century, giving good business to local odd-job carpenters. One of these was John Berry of Town End, whose descendants now run the thriving business at Kirk Mill, a company which produces over 3,000 items of furniture each week, providing good employment in the area.

Chipping to Saddle End

Walk down the lane at the side of the Corner Cafe, past the church tower and on to fork in roads. Go right and walk down, passing chair works and Grove Square and on up to go over stile on driveway opposite mill lodge. Follow right-hand fence up to go over stile.

Follow the hollow-way on, passing mounds, to go over stile in fence. Follow path to corner in wood and down to go over footbridge. Walk straight up to enter farm lane on the left of Windy Hill Farm. Follow lane down and up to pass through gate onto roadway. Pass through gate opposite and walk up to Saddle End Farm.

Saddle End 'Castlestead'

On the west side of Burnslack Brook, upon a bank at the east side of the Saddle, is an earthwork known as 'Castlestead', place of the castle/fort. The earthwork was known as such in Elizabethan times by the local farmers and landowners who thought it to be an earthen fortress of the ancient Britons.

A few years ago we went up to view this structure that is to be found above the ruin of Ward's End. It can be made out as a man-made line running along an extraordinarily steep gradient, an artificial rim high up on the steep side of the Saddle. Behind the shelter of the earthwork you are out of view to those below. But as to what purpose this structure served in ancient times I can only ponder. Excavation by spade may point to an answer.

During this exploration we surveyed the ruin of Ward's End and found in the grasses a number of window mullions and a broken 17th century doorhead. The doorhead bears ogee decoration, similar to one in Talbot Street, Chipping, with a date of 1666, and the initials P.* (O or U), possibly those of the Parker family.

In 1592, Bryan Parker had a dwelling house at Ward's End and is recorded as digging for turf on Saddle Fell. These peaty blocks would have been used to heat the dwelling and the many rutted tracks that we see running along the Saddle are possibly those made by the carts of peat diggers.

Saddle End to Fair Snape Fell/Paddy's Pole

Pass through the farmyard and follow the track on the left up onto Saddle Fell Access Area, via three stiles by gates. Continue up the old trackway till you reach a ladder-stile on the high ground. Pass over the stile and walk on through the peat hags to go over fence-stile at Wolf Fell Access Point. Follow line of fence to the left, ignoring stiles, to where the fence turns to the left (south-wards). From here walk directly on through the peat hags, past the small tarn and on picking up a slight path that leads to Paddy's Pole Cairn, the wind shelter and the Trig. Point.

Fair Snape Fell

Fair Snape has two summits, the most popular one being on the fell's western edge, and the true summit, marked by a cairn of stones, that lies just beyond the fence intersection at the Wolf Fell Access Point. The western summit affords us fine views over the Fylde and beyond Morecambe Bay to the Lakeland Fells. Below us the green meadows of Bleasdale, with her tiny scattered settlements, is laid out before us.

Fair Snape to Parlick Pike (Shorter Walk)

Follow the path along the fell's western edge, passing Nick's Chair, to the summit of Parlick Pike.

Parlick Pike

The Pike is first mentioned in 1228 as 'Pirloc', a name that could have a Scandinavian derivation: the second element 'lick' comes from the Old Norse 'lykkja' — a loop — Parlick does loop off Fair Snape and Wolf Fell, as can be clearly seen from any map. The first element could be 'pear' — again suggestive of its shape.

Parlick, in the past, has been a rallying point for local Catholics, especially during the Jacobite Rebellions of the 18th century. Tales are told of lights burning on the summit at the very dead of night, where men would set their plans against the Hanoverians. Today the Pike is a rallying point for hand-gliding enthusiasts who play on the thermals that rise up from the valley below.

Parlick Pike to Wolfen Hall

Make your way down the hill, either to Fell Foot and on to the ruin of Wildcock House via stile, or make your way down directly to the stile by the ruin. From the ruin cross the field to enter Wolfen Hall via cattle grid.

Fair Snape to Fiendsdale Head (Longer Walk)

Make your way back through the peat hags to the intersection of fences to go over the stile on the left. Follow the fence-line to the left, passing the true summit cairn, along the peaty ridge to the fence-stile at Fiendsdale Head.

Fiendsdale Head to Hazelhurst

Pass over the stile and follow the path on down to enter the lower meadow. Walk down the meadow to the farm lane and follow it to the right to Hazelhurst.

Hazelhurst

A hamlet known as Coolan once existed here, consisting of six cottages, the inhabitants making a living from wool combing and straw hat manufacture. Only the old village stocks and a deserted cottage remain today as a forlorn reminder of their industrious enterprise. The wool was transported as far as Burnley and Halifax and a packhorse bridge was built along the route at Brooks. Careful inspection of the farm walls around Hazelhurst will reveal the remains of window mullions and bottoms, dressed building stone and doorheads that came from the former settlement.

The Parkinson family are recorded as living here in 1562, and a descendant of theirs sold the estate in 1842 to William Garnett, builder, of Bleasdale Tower.

Hazelhurst to Bleasdale Circle

On leaving Hazelhurst turn right after group of trees. Follow edge of trees down to go through gateway in remains of stone wall. Walk down on a left diagonal to go over stile by the gate in the fence. Cross field on a slight left diagonal to go over stile and footbridges in far corner.

Follow track to go through gate and on up to go over stile by gate. Walk on to pass through gate onto farm lane. Left, and walk down to Vicarage Farm (ask here for permission to visit the Bronze Age village site). Enter the field on the left and walk on to pass over stile and on to go over next stile into the wooded area that contains the site.

Bleasdale Circle

For a summary of Subdivisions, climatic and environmental changes for the North of England in the Post-Glacial Period see Volume One 'Journeys through Brigantia' page 79.

This complex palisaded circular monument was discovered and partly excavated in 1898/9 and later re-excavated in 1933/5.

The inner circle was seen to comprise of a circular mound, 11m. in diameter and 1m. high, surrounded by a single-causewayed ditch floored with birch poles 10-20cm in width. Originally these would have been in the form of woven hurdles. Eleven large oak posts (their position now marked by concrete pillars) formed a circle upon the mound, with an avenue of three poles on each side across the east facing causeway.

In the centre of the mound, at a depth of 56cm, was a stone-lined cist containing two inverted cremation urns. One of the urns held a pygmy cup.

The above circular feature was surrounded by a palisade consisting of 22 large oak poles 8m. apart, between which were smaller diameter posts. The outer circle has an entrance on the south-east and what would have been a double gateway at the eastern end of the avenue.

A number of burned circular patches of soil were found within the outer circle. They were around 3-4m. in diameter, suggesting living huts, or other, destroyed by fire. These huts are assumed to be of a type consisting of a centre post, roofed with thatch with stone or earthen walls plastered with animal dung and clay over a slightly excavated round pit.

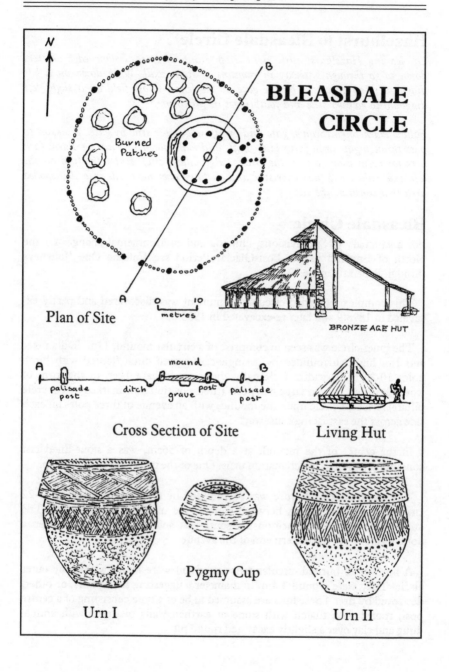

N

BLEASDALE
CIRCLE

Burned
Patches

Plan of Site

BRONZE AGE HUT

Cross Section of Site

A
palisade
post   ditch   mound
grave   post   palisade
post
B

Living Hut

Urn I

Pygmy Cup

Urn II

The cinerary urns were 21cm in height, made from local clay mixed with coarse sand. A radiocarbon date of 1810+/-90 BC (NPL-69), was obtained from timber recovered from the inner circle. If this date is correct, the well developed Pennine urns recovered from the cist are amongst the earliest collared urns to be found in Britain.

To conclude, what we have at Bleasdale is an Early Bronze Age 11 circular village site with an off-centred communal hut, surrounded by a ditch, outside of which would have been several other structures. The whole was enclosed within a palisade of oak pole construction.

Following the Indo-European custom, the dead were given to the earth inside the human habitation. The dear departed, who had been so close to the family group in life, had to remain among them in death also and share the family's joys and struggles, food and drink. While living they had enjoyed nightly rest under the roof of the communal hut, dead they sleep the eternal slumber beneath the domestic hearth.

The urns, and some of the posts, are displayed in the Harris Museum, Preston. The display is a very poor one and unenlightening, typical of most work undertaken by Lancashire County Council in this field.

Bleasdale Circle to St. Eadmer's Church

Make your way back to the farm lane and follow it on down to the church.

St. Eadmer's Church

The origins of this chapel are lost in the pages of history. The first mention of Eadmors Chapel is on a 1598 map of Lancashire.

In 1610 it was described as 'a chapel without service in the king's chase' and the stipend was said to be detained by Robert Parkinson, commissary of Richmond.

In 1689, Richard White of Chipping had the Bishop of

Chester's licence to preach in Admarsh Chapel. Because the name Admarsh was thought to be connected with the historian St. Eadmer, friend of St. Anselm, Archbishop of Canterbury during the reign of William Rufus, the church was renamed St. Eadmer when it was rebuilt in 1835.

Windows from the Elizabethan chapel can be seen today built into the west wall of the tower, and the wall to the right of the churchyard gate contains decorated stones from the early building.

Admarsh Barn

Admarsh Barn stands opposite the church, aside the old lane that leads down to Brooks packhorse bridge. The doorhead bears the initials of Robert Parkinson and the date, 1720.

ADMARSH BARN

When the adjoining lands were enclosed in 1548, the Admarsh district remained as a common pasture and turbury — where turf was collected for fuel. In 1591 the Queen was asked to divide the common pasture as it was stated to be abused by some of the inhabitants.

Brooks Packhorse Bridge

This bridge was constructed for pack-horses transporting the raw and finished wool to and from Coolan to the Pennine manufacturing areas. The bridge was erected in the mid 18th century on the site of the old river ford. The old trackway was 'lost' when the Garnetts of Bleasdale Tower built a private road and bridge through their estate.

CLOUGH HEAD BRIDGE

Brooks Packhorse Bridge

Further up the lane is Clough Head Bridge. This was built by the boys of the North Lancashire Reformatory School at Clough Head between 1858 and 1859 under the guidance of Christopher Foster, mason instructer at the school. Above the upstream arch is a dated foundation stone and above the downstream arch is a carved tablet showing the bridge's tools of construction.

The school was established by W. G. Garnett JP of Bleasdale Tower in 1857, to give one hundred boys useful employment, principally in agricultural labour. The school's farming operations brought many areas of moorland and marsh into good cultivation, resulting in what we see around us here today.

It is possible now, if you wish, to wander down the road for a drink of tea and a bite to eat at Bleasdale Post Office.

Higher Brock Mill & Post Office

The Post Office and Cafe were once the blacksmith's forge situated just down the road from Higher Brock Mill. The mill was built by Anthony Richardson.

St. Eadmer's Church to Blindhurst

Walk down, past the school, to go over cattle grid and into the field on the left to follow left-hand fence to go over stile by edge of wood. Go through wood heading slightly to the right to go over stile. Cross the field on a slight right diagonal to pass through gateway.

Walk on to join lane and along to cattle-grid to go right following left-hand fence and brook, on to go over footbridge and through gateway. Walk upstream to edge of trees and on up to go through gateway in front of you. Walk on, then follow left-hand fence up to pass through gate. Follow track up to enter farmyard by two gates. Pass the barn and house (steps of spiral staircase built into wall on right) then through gate and around to the front of the house.

Blindhurst

Blindhurst presents an interesting frontage, with its mullioned and transomed windows and pillared Georgian doorway, all reflecting the wealth of its builder, Richard Edward Parkinson, whose initials appear on a tablet above the doorway with the date, 1731.

Christopher Parkinson of Blindhurst was a deputy steward of the Forest of Bowland in 1611, under the Parkers of Browsholme.

Anthony Parkinson of Blindhurst (1666-1728) joined the Franciscans at Douay, taking the name of Cuthbert and thus forgoing his rights of inheritance of Blindhurst, and was sent on the English Mission in 1695. As well as being a missionary he became a Franciscan historian, his 'Collectanea Anglo-Minoriticain' being published in 1726. He went on to become a Provincial of the Order.

The rear of the house has mullioned windows and built into the corner of the barn wall are steps from a spiral staircase, re-used as quoins. Inside the house is a fine corbelled mantlepiece and corner cupboard.

The place-name 'Blindhurst' means 'a dark or obscure wood', recalling the forest of long ago.

Blindhurst to Wolfen Hall

From front of house walk back out of the farmyard to the right of the house and on up to the right to pass through gate. Follow wall round to join a grassy trackway and on, across stream and up to the left to pass over fence-stile. Walk up to the right to go over clough and over fence-stile.

Follow path on over the hillside to Fell Foot Farm. From rear of house follow the path eastwards, and over onto the right of gully to pass over fence-stile at ruin. Walk down to the left, then over to the right to cattle-grid. Follow trackway on to Wolfen Hall.

Wolfen Hall

Wolfen Hall was once the old manor house of Chipping, being then home of John de Knoll of Chippindale and later passing by marriage to Roger, third son of Robert Shireburn of Stonyhurst. The Shireburns, along with the Hoghton family, became the largest landowners in the district, both holding rival courts in the village.

In St. Bartholomew's Church there was the Shireburn Chantry, also known as Wolfhouse Quire. This was founded in 1519 by Roger Shireburn and used as a burial place for the Shireburns up till the late 17th century.

Wolfen Hall to Chipping

Walk away from the front of the house to pass over cattle-grid and follow farm lane on to above lower house. Cross the field on the left to pass over fence-stile. Follow woodside path down to the right, over old mill-race to pass through gate. Follow roadway down from the old mill lodge, over bridge and up to junction. Follow the roadway down to the right to Chipping.

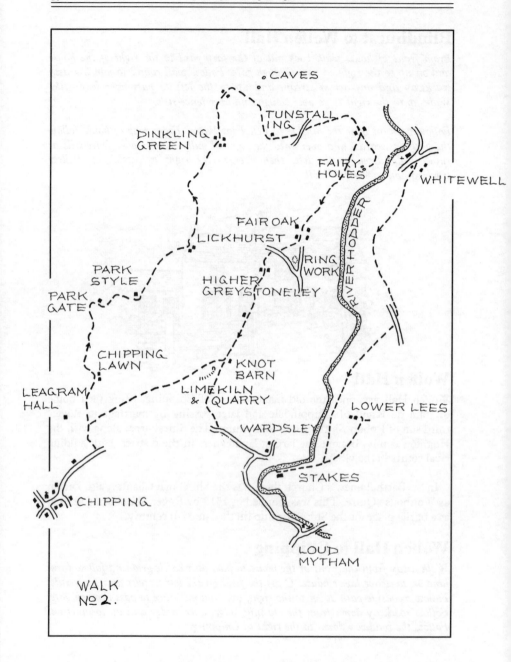

CAVES

TUNSTALL ING

DINKLING GREEN

FAIRY HOLES

WHITEWELL

FAIR OAK

LICKHURST

RING WORK

RIVER HODDER

PARK STYLE

HIGHER GREYSTONELEY

PARK GATE

CHIPPING LAWN

KNOT BARN

LIME KILN & QUARRY

LOWER LEES

LEAGRAM HALL

WARDSLEY

STAKES

CHIPPING

LOUD MYTHAM

WALK No 2.

Walk 2

ON LIMESTONE ABOVE THE WHITEWELL GORGE

8 miles, 5 hours.

MAP: *O.S. SD 64/74 PATHFINDER*

LUNCH: *Packed Lunch & Flask*

START: *Car Park opposite church, Chipping.*

On this walk we wander through an old deer park to discover the 'lost' hamlet of Dinkling Green, hidden away by limestone knolls. Then on to view the Hodder Valley from Tunstall Ing, in my mind, the finest view over the valley. After exploring caves once known to early man we return by way of Greystoneley along ancient lanes and tracks that today feel only the walkers tread.

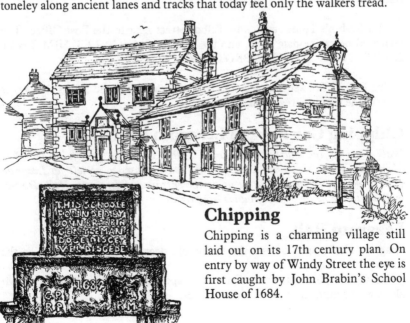

Chipping

Chipping is a charming village still laid out on its 17th century plan. On entry by way of Windy Street the eye is first caught by John Brabin's School House of 1684.

Chipping

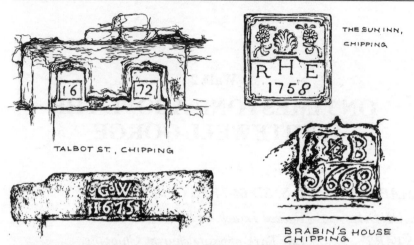

Brabin was a local dyer and cloth merchant who acquired his wealth through the 'putting out' system of textile manufacture. In his will of April 1683, he granted monies for the establishing of a school in the village. This grant also provided for the uniforms of sixteen pupils, shelter for the local poor through the building of almshouses and the cost of three boys to be apprenticed to a trade annually.

John Brabin's House stands in Talbot Street next to the Post Office. The doorhead bears the date 1688, and the inscription reads: LET HIM THAT LOVETH GOD LOVE HIS BROTHER ALSO.

The Post Office sells a good selection of local books and across the way is some of the best ice-cream in Lancashire.

Chipping Car Park to Leagram Hall

Walk on past the church to go down Talbot Street to go left at the War Memorial. Walk along the road, past the lodge house, to go left up Leagram Hall driveway. Follow the drive up to the entrance of Leagram Hall. Do not walk up to the house as the grounds are private.

Leagram Hall

Leagram Hall stands on the site of the old deer park lodge, known as the Lawn.

During the 16th century a Catholic chapel was established at the Lawn along with a number of priest hiding places.

Leagram Hall

Those were dark days for members of the Catholic faith, both Leagram and Wolfen Hall hid priests during that time of persecution. It is reputed that Edmund Arrowsmith (executed at Lancaster, August 18th, 1628) occasionally ministered at Leagram Hall.

From 1556 up until the late 17th century, the Lawn was used as a dower house of the Shireburns of Stonyhurst. The house was later passed to Thomas Weld and became home of the Jesuits of Liege. Traces of the old chapel still remain in the west wing. The present Gothik chapel was built by Weld in around 1856.

Leagram was once a great deer park surrounded by a dyke, traces of which can still be made out today. Within the park grew many large oaks, but when disparked in 1556, no deer were left and the few oaks which stood were found to be unfit for building.

Leagram Hall to Dinkling Green

Continue on to Chipping Lawn Farm and follow the lane on, over cattle-grid, to go right at the junction on to Park Gate (with the bridge and waterfalls this makes a delightful setting). Pass front of house and go through gateway to follow trackway on, through next gate, following right hand fence to go through gate on right.

Follow track down to the ruin of the 17th century Park Style. Follow farm track on, through gates, to Lickhurst. Follow lane down to go over footbridge and on up to go over fence stile. Walk on to go through gateway and on to go through next gateway. Follow left-hand wall/fence on around the field to go through gateway onto track. Right, and walk down to enter the settlement of Dinkling Green.

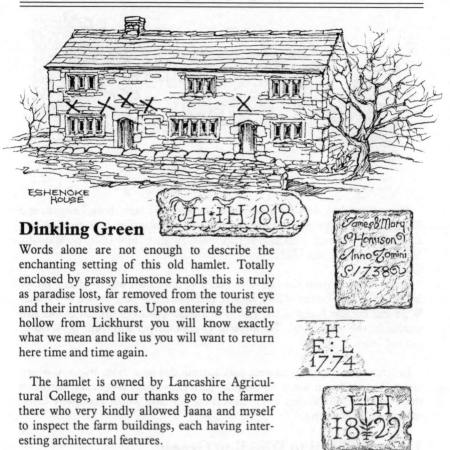

ESHENOKE
HOUSE

Dinkling Green

Words alone are not enough to describe the
enchanting setting of this old hamlet. Totally
enclosed by grassy limestone knolls this is truly
as paradise lost, far removed from the tourist eye
and their intrusive cars. Upon entering the green
hollow from Lickhurst you will know exactly
what we mean and like us you will want to return
here time and time again.

The hamlet is owned by Lancashire Agricultural College, and our thanks go to the farmer
there who very kindly allowed Jaana and myself
to inspect the farm buildings, each having interesting architectural features.

The field barn bears a fine inscribed datestone of 1738 recording the tenancy
of the Harrison family; the Harrisons are recorded as farmers at Beatrix and
Hareden in the Forest Court lists of 1323. The Harrisons replaced the Bleasdale family who farmed here in the 17th century.

On entering the farmyard notice the stone head above a doorway on the left.
The barn opposite has a room at the rear lit by a small round-headed window,

said once to have served as a chapel for the hamlet. The barn is dated 1774 E.H.L. Across the yard the cottage on the left is dated 1829 J.H., which complements one at the bottom of the yard dated 1818 JH*IH. The building on the right was once an old schoolhouse and inspection of the inside revealed a large pair of oaken crucks.

The jewel at Dinkling Green is to be found at the bottom of the yard, for here stands the solid 17th century building of Eshenoke House. It displays two Tudor doorheads and low mullioned windows. This was once the home of the Bleasdale family whose initials are loosely carved on one of the window bottoms. If any building deserved restoration to a purposeful building then it is this fine edifice.

Dinkling Green to New Laund Farm

Go through the small gate between the garden wall of the major detached house and the modern farm building to cross the field to go over stile to the left of the gateway. Follow fence over on the right to go through gateway in fence. Ford stream by footbridge and walk on into Higher Fence Wood farmyard.

Follow farm lane to Tunstall Ing. After passing the house come off the lane and into the field on the left. Walk down the field heading for the limestone outcrop to go over fence stile onto road. Pass through the gateway on the left opposite and walk down bearing right to pass through gate. Follow right-hand fence to go through gate and follow rutted trackway to New Laund.

NEW LAUND

New Laund

New Laund was a keeper's house in the days of the great forest, and the inhabitants used stepping stones set in the bed of the Hodder to reach the manor house at Whitewell.

The Hipping stones have long gone but it is still possible to cross the river at this spot by walking on a diagonal down river on the wide bed of river-stones below the Inn at Whitewell.

New Laund to Fairy Holes

Walk through the farmyard, past the farmhouse to go through the right-hand gate. Walk up onto the banking on the right to find a pathway. Follow the pathway up to where it bends down. Leave the path and head up the hillside, working your way up to the left to find a limestone outcrop on which the caves are located. After viewing retrace your steps back to New Laund.

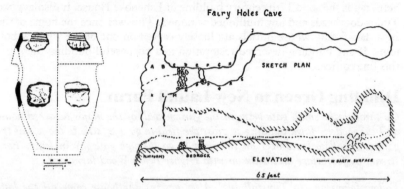

Fairy Holes Caves

Sited on a shelf on the south-east face of an outcrop of limestone are three cave openings. The larger cave is 65 ft. long, 6 ft. high and 10 ft. wide, and leads to a large round chamber.

In 1946, an excavation was carried out on the site by the archaeologist Reginald C. Musson. In front of the larger cave is a flat platform on which evidence of Bronze Age daily life was found. This included animal bones, a pebble pounder (used to extract marrow from bones) and shards of a food vessel/urn.

All that survived of this tripartite collared urn was a large rim-collar shard, two fragments displaying neck/shoulder/body elements and five smaller pieces, probably from the base of the body. This is the only collared urn to have been found in a cave in Lancashire. Its tripartite Pennine form assigns it to an early Bronze Age date.

Aerial photography has identified a number of possible settlement sites in the area between Dinkling Green and the Hodder at Whitewell and in the area around Whitmore below Totridge Fell. The largest of these sites is at Fair Oak farm.

New Laund to Fair Oak Farm

Go through the gate on the left of the barn and follow the track up to go over stile by gate between left side of hill and the wood. Follow track around the back of the hill to go over wall-stile down on left. Follow right-hand wall to go over stile. On a slight right-diagonal cross the field to farm track. Walk on into Fair Oak. The Old Coach House is up on the right. The farm house is on the left, and the Gunnary Barn is at the bottom of the farmyard. Make your way to the Gunnary.

Fair Oak Farm

The old vaccary of Fair Oak, locally called 'Farrick', has had many past names — Fair del Holme and Fairdockhouse are but two. Sadly, the old Fair Oak House no longer stands — a modern bungalow now occupies the site.

An oil painting of the house, painted in the early 17th century, once hung in the hallway of the farm house, but this was wrongly placed in a Longridge auction by the previous owner.

The Old Coach House stands as a reminder of those bygone days, restored to a high standard and a credit to the owners. On the easterly gable end, flanked by a dove cote, is a stone tablet with the following inscription: JOHN PARKINSON, DOROTHY HIS WIFE, AND THOMAS HIS SON, 1716. A door lintel above an old toilet on the south side bears the date 1664, and nearby stands the weight from an old cheese press.

Inside the farmhouse are two rather grand stone fireplaces, one of which has a fire-head that is a re-used doorhead with a date of 1720. An old water pump once stood in the yard; this bore the initials of John Clince Parker and the date 1819.

The barn at Fair Oak is a robust-looking building and is known as the 'Gunnary', reference to the role played by the Parkinsons in the Jacobite Rebellion of 1715 and again in 1745. Many people in the area supported the Jacobite cause, and in Chaigley an Hanoverian

FAIR OAK FARM

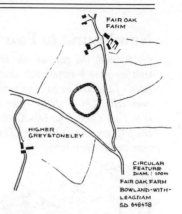

barracks was established and the region placed under Martial Law. From this seat the soldiery sallied forth to harass the lands and humble abodes of the outlaws.

The Singlehursts lived at Fair Oak in 1422. Old records tell us of one Christopher Harris, who married Mary, daughter and heir of Robert Singlehurst of Fair Oak. Harris took the king's side during the Civil War, and as a 'recusant and delinquent' had his estate sequestered in 1654.

Recent aerial photography has identified a large circular earthwork at Fair Oak. It has a surrounding ditch and bank enclosing a raised circular mound of approximately 100m in diameter. It is thought that this feature may relate to Bronze Age activity in the area, and could possibly be a village site.

Fair Oak to Knot Barn

Go through the gate on the left of the Gunnary and cross the field to the far right corner to go over stiles onto roadway. Pass over stile opposite and cross the field to go over stile onto farm trackway. Follow the trackway on through Higher Greystoneley and down to the ford (what a wonderful little wood this is, take note of the many mosses growing on the old walls). Cross the ford and follow the trackway on past Lower Greystoneley to Knot Barn and the limekiln by the old quarry.

HIGHER GREYSTONELEY

Greystoneley

Greystoneley is first mentioned in 1462, and the name means 'pasture by the Grey Stone', the 'Grey Stone' possibly being an old boundary stone.

Higher Greystoneley is a solidly-built farmhouse dated 1873, with the initials J.W. In the lower field stands an old stone crushing machine. This was used for crushing the kiln-fired limestone before spreading it on the fields or mixing it as a mortar. Near Knot Barn are the old limestone quarries complete with a large lime kiln.

Knot Barn to Chipping

Walk on passing the open mouth of the kiln and after passing the quarry cross the field directly to go over a stile by gate in far fence. Walk down to the stream bearing slightly to the right to go over footbridge (notice the line of an old mill-race that once fed Leagram Mill). Cross the stream and walk on to the holly tree. Now follow right-hand hedge/fence, over four stiles to cross a field to Leagram Hall driveway. Walk down the driveway to roadway. Right, and follow road on to Chipping.

St. Bartholomew's Church, Chipping

A church was established here sometime before 1230, but little is known of the early foundation. For the most part the present fabric represents the major restoration of 1873, but a few interesting pieces remain from former ages. The oldest of these is the cross base which stands next to a 16th century chest of Belgian origin. This base lost its position and shaft some time after 1610. A 14th century piscina can be found in a recess in the south wall of the sanctuary. The font is by far the church's finest piece. It dates from 1520, supposedly the gift of Bradley of Bradley Hall, whose initials appear on one of the shields.

The devices on the other shields represent the instruments of the Passion: the nails, the hammer, the pincers and the scourges. There are two blank shields whose designs have been obliterated — these were possibly the five wounds of Christ and the Sacred Heart. Around the base are the inverted letters A M G P D T — Ave Maria Gratia Piena Dominus Tecum (St. Luke. Ch. 1. Verse 28).

In the churchyard stands a sundial upon stone steps with the date 1708 and the initials of the churchwardens of that time.

A Bronze Age burial mound was uncovered during road and building work to the north of the church in c.1770. An urn was revealed, marked with a lozenge decoration and containing fragments of bone. The site is remembered today by the name Grove Row, the site of the old workhouse.

CHIPPING

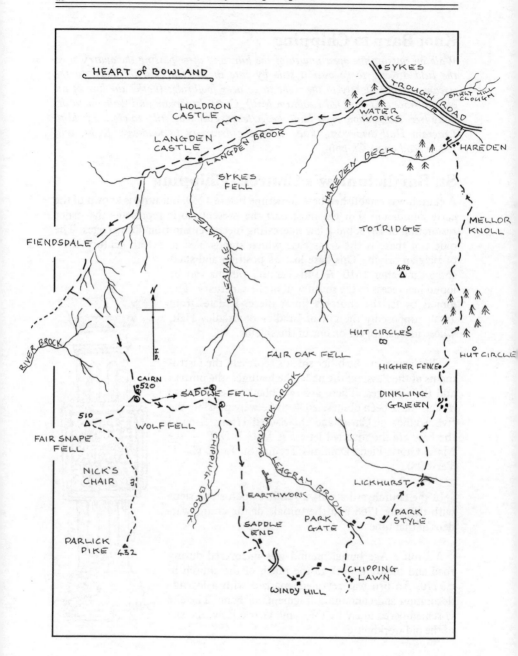

HEART of BOWLAND

SYKES

TROUGH ROAD

SMELT MILL CLOUGH

HOLDRON CASTLE

WATER WORKS

LANGDEN CASTLE

LANGDEN BROOK

HAREDEN

SYKES FELL

HAREDEN BECK

MELLOR KNOLL

TOTRIDGE

FIENDSDALE

496 △

RIVER BROOK

N

HUT CIRCLES

FAIR OAK FELL

HUT CIRCLE

HIGHER FENCE

CAIRN 520

SADDLE FELL

DINKLING GREEN

510 △

WOLF FELL

FAIR SNAPE FELL

CHIPPING BROOK

BURDSLACK BROOK

LEAGRAM BROOK

LICKHURST

NICK'S CHAIR

EARTHWORK

PARK STYLE

PARLICK PIKE 432

SADDLE END

PARK GATE

CHIPPING LAWN

WINDY HILL

Walk 3

HEART OF BOWLAND

15 miles, 7 hours.

MAPS: *O.S. SD 64/74, SD 44/54 & SD 65/75.*

LUNCH: *Flask & Packed Lunch.*
                          Tea is available at Lickhurst Farm.

START: *Langden Car Park.*

The lengthy Langden Valley approach to the summit of Fair Snape Fell is a walk that you never want to end, such is the sense of solitude and well-being provided by the wilderness here. The ling and fern-clothed valley sides soar steeply upwards and one feels drawn into the very heart of the wild Bowland hills, following the river on and on to the peat-hag watershed of Fiendsdale.

The return, high above the Loud and Hodder, is a joy of rustic landscapes; green meadows and rolling hills with here and there a friendly farmstead, coupled with good company this makes for a rewarding and enjoyable day out.

Langden Car Park to Langden Castle
Follow the conifer-lined lane to the lovely setting of Langden Intake Waterworks. From here continue along the stony track up the valley to Langden Castle.

Langden Castle
A stone Axe Hammer, with an hourglass perforation, was found in Langden Beck in 1988. This valley route through Bowland would have been known to those Bronze Age settlers at Bleasdale and Dinkling Green.

LANGDEN CASTLE

Langden Castle stands in an oasis of green at the foot of Bleadale Water. Though only a simple shepherd's hut today, I suspect that it once served as a shooting lodge in the 19th century — the gothic windows and doorway point to something other than a farm building. A small path leads up Bleadale to the top of Saddle Fell, but this is not a right of way.

Langden Castle to Fiendsdale Head Stile

Follow the stony track on a short way and leave the track to follow the waymarked path (yellow tipped poles) to ford the brook above the confluence with Fiendsdale Water. Follow the narrow path up the ling-clad slopes (looking back to gain fine views from time to time) and through the peat hags (marked by cairns) to a fence-stile at Fiendsdale Head.

It is now possible to visit Bleasdale below by using the directions given in Walk 1.

Fiendsdale Head to Fair Snape Fell/Paddy's Pole

Do not pass over the stile, but follow the fence to the left for some distance to the true summit cairn of Fair Snape Fell and on to pass over fence-stile on the right. Walk past the Wolf Fell access stile and follow the line of the fence on to where it turns to the left. From here walk directly on through the peat hags, past the small tarn (on your left) and on to pick up a slight path that leads on to Paddy's Pole/Trig. Pt. summit.

Fair Snape Fell to Dinkling Green

Make your way back to the last stile we came over and pass over the Wolf Fell access stile on the right (on the way notice the old War Department marker stone — W D No27, reminding us that the Bowland Fells were once a military training ground — unexploded shells still litter the area so be careful and report any strange object).

Follow path that runs by fence on the left on through the peat hags to fence-ladder stile near junction of fences. Pass over stile and follow path down to the right to next ladder-stile. From here follow the path down to the left to follow the old track-ways down to go over stile by gate.

Follow track down (W D No34) to pass through two more gateways to enter Saddle End Farm. Pass through the farmyard and follow the lane down to the roadway. Pass through the gate opposite to follow track on, past Windy Hill Farm and on, past Birchen Lee Farm (JW 1867) to follow the lane that leads to the left, just above Chipping Lawn Farm, to Park Gate (CW 1863 — Weld). Walk past front of house to go through gateway to follow trackway on, through next gate, following right-hand fence to go through gate on right.

Follow track down to ruin of 17th century Park Style and on, through gates and on over to Lickhurst Farm (Teas available).

Follow the lane down to go over footbridge on left at bend. Walk up to pass over stile and on up to go over stile by gate and on to pass through gateway. Walk down to the left to pass through gateway. Walk down to the right, through gateway and follow left-hand fence on to pass through gate onto trackway. Follow trackway on to enter the tiny hamlet of Dinkling Green.

Dinkling Green to Hareden

Go through the small gate between major house garden wall and modern cattle shed and cross the field to go over stile on left of gateway. Walk on to fence and follow it on to go through gateway in fence. Cross the stream by footbridge and on to pass through farmyard onto lane. Follow lane on a short way to go left at junction. At the second group of hen-houses leave the lane as it bends to the left to follow the footpath on the right to enter wood via gate. Follow woodland track on to leave via gate.

Follow path on, over hillside stream and on to pass over stile by small gate (look back at the view of the Hodder Valley). Follow path on to go over wall-stile near gate. Walk over to the right with Mellor Knoll summit ahead to drop down to the left to pass through gate at junction in walls (waymarked posts). Follow left-hand wall down to pass over stile by gate and on down to enter Hareden via footbridge.

Hareden

Today dogs herald our arrival at the Hareden Kennels breaking the accustomed stillness of this hidden valley. The buildings date back to the 17th century when the Harrison and Knowle families farmed here.

The farmstead was first established by the monks of Kirkstall Abbey as a cattle farm (vaccary) and tenanted by the Harrisons.

Hareden to Langden Car Park

Follow the farm lane down to the roadway, then follow the Trough road to the left to the Langden car park.

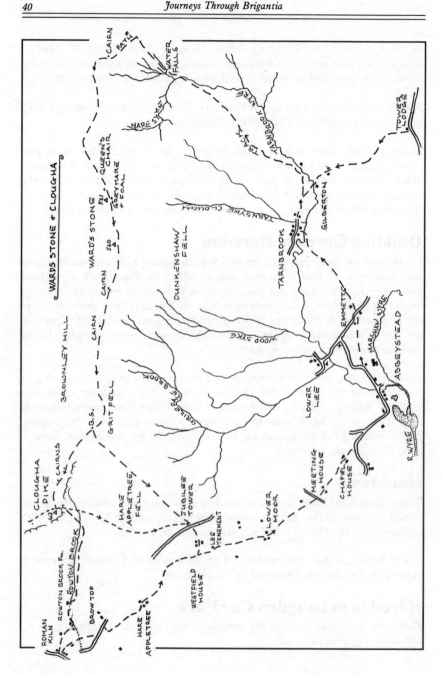

Walk 4

WARD'S STONE & CLOUGHA PIKE

19½ miles, 9 to 10 hours.

MAP: *O.S. SD 45/55 PATHFINDER 659*

LUNCH: *Packed Lunch & Flask.*

START: *Tower Lodge, Trough of Bowland.*

Today we climb Bowland's highest hill, Ward's Stone, and walk the length of its spine to attain views over Lancaster from the rock peak of Clougha Pike. For many years this highland was out-of-bounds for the general public, but, thanks to the citizens of the County of Lancashire, access paths have been negotiated with the major landowners.

These routes are closed only during the grouse shooting season — August 12th and on up to ten additional days to the end of the season on December 12th. Camping is prohibited, no fires are to be lit and dogs are strictly not allowed.

Tower Lodge to Ward's Stone Access Path

Pass through the gate and walk up the track to pass through upper gate and on to guide-post on left before wall bends to the right. Walk to the left to old cheese-press weight. Walk up the field on a left diagonal, over old low wall and on to pass over two fence-stiles and a wall-stile. Follow wall down to the right, through gateway and on down, over wall-stile and on down to pass through gate on left. Walk down to pass barns via gates and follow track on to Gilberton Farm to go over footbridge on right. Walk on to follow farm lane on to join the Access Path.

Access Track to Waterfalls

Follow shooter's track up Tarnbrook Fell, and on when it becomes a pathway to the head of the falls.

Tarnbrook Wyre Waterfalls

I only do the 'Ward's Stone Walk' in the dry summer months or in mid January when a good frost is down, for the route from here on can be dreadful as the swampy peat hags and the rough terrain make for very poor going in times of wet weather. But don't be put off — in dry or frosty conditions the going is pure joy.

The waterfalls at the head of the Tarnbrook Wyre watershed make for a good first stop, the cascading waters provide a surprise setting in this rough terrain. Notice the large stone with an inverted 'M' deeply carved into it — I have no idea as to its purpose.

Waterfalls to Ward's Stone

Cross the falls and follow path on and upstream, across small flat stone bridge and on upstream (yellow marked stakes) to go over fence-stile on ridge. (Wolfhole Crag over on the right). Follow fence to the left to go over fence-stile and on following wall/fence/wall boundary, over Grey Crag (large gritstone boulders) to pass over fence-stile (we saw a young fox sitting on a wall here). Follow fence to the left to go over fence-stile at Queen's Chair (W.M. bench-marked weathered stone). Walk on to cairn on rock near summit Trig. Pt. Follow path on (westerly) to Ward's Stone Trig. Pt.

Ward's Stone

At 1836 ft. (561m), Ward's Stone is the highest point on the Bowland Fells giving one wide views over Morecambe Bay, the Lakeland Fells and the high peaks of the Yorkshire Dales. The highest point is the easterly Trig. Point near some wind-carved boulders known as the Grey Hare and Foal (561m). The westerly Trig. Point (560m) stands by the huge boulder known as Ward's Stone. Various crevices in the boulders provide for a second resting place before the moorland track to Clougha.

Ward's Stone to Clougha Pike

Follow path on (westerly), across the shooter's road and on up Grit Fell to go over fence-stile (a path on the left here leads directly down to Jubilee Tower). Notice the boundary stone (S 1263 yds).

Follow the fence/wallside path on to go over fence-stile. Follow the path over the moor, and pass over Clougha and fence-stile to Clougha Pike shelter and Trig. Pt.

Clougha Pike

From Clougha Pike we obtain our first major view of the Lancashire and Cumbria coastline with Blackpool Tower and Heysham Power Station dominating the skyline. A stone shelter lends for another rest stop before the short decent to Quernmore.

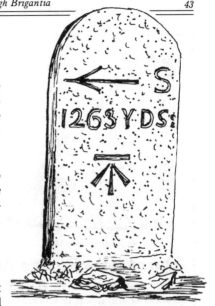

Clougha Pike to Quernmore Roman Kilns

From the Trig. Pt. take the path south and follow it down and around to the west (a path leads over the moor to go over a fence-stile and on down to Jubilee Tower) to go over stream and on to go through gate and on down to pass through next two gates.

Rooten Brook Farm

Follow path on down to enter Rooten Brook farmyard via gate. Pass through farmyard (datestone T.I.D. 1695) and down the farm lane, across stream and on to go right down old lane at fork to go through gate.

Walk down to driveway and follow it on to Rigg Lane roadway. Left, and walk on to pass through gate on left. Walk over to the right, the kiln is over the wall in the private wooded area.

AL(A)E SEBVSIA(NAE)

No. 1.—13 inches by 12.   No. 2.—14 inches by 9.

Quernmore Roman Kilns

Quernmore lies about three miles to the south-east of the Roman Fort of Lancaster and it was in Quernmore Park that a Roman Pottery Kiln was first discovered in the 18th century. The site yielded pottery and roofing tiles relating to the 3rd century AD. The tiles bore the stamp of the Ala Sebosiana, a unit stationed at Lancaster in the mid-third century. This site is located a mile to the north of where we are now at SD 619521.

The Quernmore site has so far yielded two kilns and pottery dating from the late 1st to 3rd century AD, together with evidence of iron-roasting, which points to an industrial complex of some size.

The first kiln was in near perfect condition and was built into a small hill, so that the hill itself baked with heat and acted as the rear and side walls of the kiln. This kiln was of an up-draught type, having a stone oven floor, lined with clay and pierced at intervals with vent holes through which entered the hot gasses produced by a wood fire in the fire chamber underneath.

The second kiln is of a different construction, not having a permanent floor and showing some signs of having been converted, possibly in the Roman period, for lime burning. The pottery found in this second kiln was of approximately the same date as that found in the first kiln. No evidence of accommodation or administrative building have so far been found.

Roman Kiln to Hare Appletree

Walk up the hill to Low Pleasant Farm via gate. Follow farm lane up to top lane via gate. Cross the lane and walk up the field, through large wall opening and on to the roadway via stile by gate. Left, and walk up the road to go right, down Brow Top lane to go over stile by gate on left. Walk up the field on slight right-diagonal to follow fence over the hill to go through gate onto lane. Follow lane on to Hare Appletree.

Hare Appletree

The Victoria Jubilee Tower, that stands by the roadside below Clougha Pike, was erected in 1887 at the expense of Jane Harrison of Hare Appletree.

The tiny hamlet of Hare Appletree (meaning Grey Appletree) is first mentioned in 1323, and it has grown little since that time.

A careful look above doorways and on the walls of some of the farmbuildings here will reveal a number of datestones from the 17th and 18th centuries. Two of those I recorded are pictured here.

I am often asked why I include so many datestones and doorheads in my books. The answer is simply that I wish to draw attention to the great variety of type and style in the region. Many now adorn simple farmsteads that were once the family seats of Yeoman families. Datestones tell us when a house was built, and often who built it. They recall a settlement pattern of a former rural age, and display workmanship often of a localised nature that reflects the taste, often corrupted, of higher society.

Today many are time-worn, some have been lost and others defaced. My work is an attempt to record and bring to public attention their value to our Historical and Architectural Heritage as well as the simple form of beauty and wonder that they hold in themselves.

Hare Appletree to Abbeystead

From the bottom farmyard, pass through gate and over ford to walk to the right and up to go over fence-stile. Walk on veering up to the left to go over fence-stile hidden in gully near end of line of trees. Cross stream and walk directly on to go over corner wall-stile. Follow left-hand wall on, over fence-stile and on to farm lane via wall-stile near gate. Follow lane directly on to pass front of Lee Tenement to go over garden wall-stile. Walk directly on to pass over corner fence-stile. Follow fence on, over fence-stile and on to go through field-gate on left. Follow fence on to go over wall-stile at Lower Moor Head. Pass through gate opposite and follow left-hand boundary on, over wall-stile and on to go over stile by gate.

Follow track on, through field-gate and directly on to go through gate onto roadway. Follow farm lane ahead to go over wall-stile by side of house (Meeting House Farm). Follow path on to go over footbridge and directly on veering up to the left to go through gate (waymarked). Cross field on a left diagonal to pass through gate and on to enter Chapel House farmyard. Pass through lower gate and walk on down the field on the left to go over fence-stile between trees and on to roadway via gate. Follow the road to the left on down to Abbeystead.

Abbeystead

There are a number of good low-level walks to be had around Abbeystead and a book I strongly recommend is one by Ian O. Brodie 'Walking from Garstang and in Wyresdale', published by Carnegie Publishing Ltd, Preston.

The place-name Abbeystead means 'the site of the Abbey', preserving the memory of a house of Cistercian monks in Wyresdale, founded by monks from Furness Abbey in the reign of Henry II (1154-1189) but soon removed. In 1323 it is recorded as a vaccary (cow farm) belonging to the Abbey of Furness.

Many of the houses in Abbeystead are built in an Elizabethan style and lend great charm to their surroundings. Between these are a number of 17th century survivals; one in the centre of the village is dated 1677 with the initials I.D. & N.D.E., and Catshaw Hall is dated 1678. Abbeystead House, centre of the Duke of Westminster's Bowland Estate, was built in 1886 by the Earl of Sefton, again in the Elizabethan style.

Christ Church is the Shepherd's church. It was rebuilt in 1733 from local stone. Inside the porch are wooden bars with iron hooks where the shepherds once hung their crooks and lanterns. On display inside is a Geneva Bible of 1599. The pulpit is Jacobean in design and dated 1684.

Abbeystead to Tarnbrook

Pass through the village and up the steep Strait Lane to pass through gate and garden of corner house to go over fence-stile. Walk directly on across the field to go through gate set back on right of waymarked gate. Follow boundary on to step over fence below Higher Emmetts and on to go over fence-stile. Cross road and walk up farm lane opposite to go over stile on right.

Follow left-hand boundary on to go over fence-stile near corner and follow right-hand fence on to go over next fence-stile. Cross the field diagonally to go over corner fence-stile. Walk on to right of barn to follow right-hand fence/hedgerow on, over wall-stile and on following wall/fence to go over stile onto old lane. Left, then right, to go over stile. Cross field to go over next two stiles. Walk on to go over stile by gate. Cross the bridge and walk on into Tarnbrook.

Tarnbrook

Tarnbrook is a 'closed village', being part of the Duke of Westminster's Bowland Estate. A Mountain Rescue Post is sited here manned by a LCC ranger. At one time the village comprised twenty-five houses, with most of the tenants being employed as hatmakers.

Tarnbrook to Tower Lodge

Follow village road on, past Mountain Rescue Post to go through 'Gilberton' gate on left at Access Sign. Follow track on to pass over footbridge at Gilberton. Walk on to follow path to barns via gates. Pass through gate and follow path up, through gate and on up, over wall-stile and on, through gateway and on to go over wall-stile on left. Cross field on a right-diagonal to go over next two stiles and on down to pass through gate. Follow track down to Tower Lodge.

Walk 5

ONCE DEER DID ROAM
AND ROMANS MARCH

9 & 5 miles, 5 or 3 hours.

MAP: *O.S. SD 64/74 PATHFINDER*

LUNCH: *Packed lunch & flask*

START: *Whitewell Hotel*

This walk takes us into an ancient parkland below and above Whitewell within which lie some rewarding rural dwellings ranging from the rustic Lees and Stakes to the country grandeur of Browsholme. Cutting through this arcadia is the old Roman highway from Ribchester to Overborough. Long gone the Legions pounding tread, now cows and walkers roam here instead.

Whitewell Chapel

A chapel was established at Whitewell in c.1400 by Walter de Urswyck, Keeper of the Royal Forest of Bowland.

Urswyck was Constable of Richmond and Keeper of the 'New Forest' — a wide tract of virgin ground, moor and scroggland reaching from the

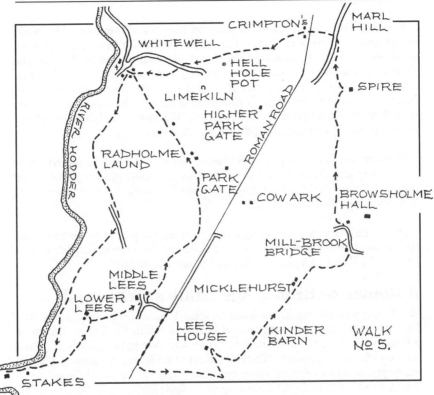

MARL HILL

CRIMPTON'S

WHITEWELL

HELL HOLE POT

SPIRE

LIMEKILN

HIGHER PARK GATE

ROMAN ROAD

RIVER HODDER

RADHOLME LAUND

PARK GATE

COW ARK

BROWSHOLME HALL

MILL-BROOK BRIDGE

MIDDLE LEES

LOWER LEES

MICKLEHURST

LEES HOUSE

KINDER BARN

WALK Nº 5.

STAKES

north bank of the Swale to
Stainmoor and the Tees, and
westward across Arkengarthdale
to the Pennines.

John of Gaunt, Duke of Lancaster, and Earl of Richmond,
granted Walter de Urswyck an
annuity of forty pounds a year
out of the manors of Catterick
and Forcet, for his valiant serv-
ices at the Battle of Navarre
in support of the noblesse of
Knighthood. His effigy rests
on an altar-tomb in Catterick
Church.

Records inform us that in 1422, extensive repairs and alterations were made to the manor house and chapel; the chapel received a new roof and good windows. After the Reformation the chapel was dedicated to St. Michael the Archangel and received the revenue formerly given to a chapel of that name which once stood in the grounds of Clitheroe Castle. The Clitheroe chapel had been abandoned and finally demolished during the Reformation. A curate from Whalley would preach once a month at Whitewell and rights of marriage and burial were performed at Clitheroe parish church.

The drawing shows the post-Reformation chapel and not the enlarged building we see today that was built in 1818. Only the small window in the boiler house on the north side of the chapel displays Perpendicular tracery and is all that remains of the chapel of 1422.

Inside the chapel a good example of a Jacobean pulpit can be viewed along with a fine tapestry that depicts Christ's descent from the Cross, based on a painting by Rubins which is on view in Antwerp Cathedral.

A Roman or Bronze Age Camp at Whitewell

W. Thompson Watkin in his book 'Roman Lancashire' (1883), states that "according to Lewis's 'Topographical Dictionary' (7th Ed. 1849), remains of a Roman camp existed at Whitewell." And Whitaker in his History of Whalley records that "opposite Whitewell Keeper's House, remains of a small encampment and a cairn of stones containing kist vaen and a skeleton" were found. Could both authors be referring to the same site?

The Keeper's Cottage is now the Inn at Whitewell and nothing remains today of the site mentioned above.

In 1984 a large carved-out round stone was found in the River Hodder near to the Inn. Upon inspection, archaeologists have declared the stone to be mortar for the grinding of food grains and date it to the Bronze Age period. The mortar is now known as 'The Whitewell Stone', and is safely housed within the hotel.

THE WHITEWELL STONE.

Whitewell to Stakes

Walk up past the Village Hall to go up the steps on right at footpath sign. Pass through small gateway opposite and up to the trackway on the right of the house. Right, and follow trackway to go through top gate. Follow right-hand wall to pass through kissing-gate. Follow right-hand fence, over stile, and on (notice the line of the old Deer Park ditch running across the fields below) to go through another kissing-gate. Follow fence on to pass through kissing-gate and cross field to go through gateway onto the road at the edge of trees.

Walk along the road to go over stile by gate on right. Cross the field on a left-diagonal to corner of wood, here follow fence down to go over stile. Walk along the line of old trackway to go down to ford the stream. Go over the stile on the right, then left, and go through corner gate. Walk up the hillside to the right of the ditch, to go through gate onto farm lane. Turn right and walk on to Stakes.

Stakes

Stakes Farm stands in the south-west corner of the ancient Domesday manor of Sotelie, now known as the Lees. The farm takes its unusual name from the palisade of oak pailings which enclosed the old Leagram Deer Park on the opposite bank of the Hodder.

In Cromwellian times a ferryboat existed here, the ferryman living in a stone dwelling adjoining the garden of the farm. Of course the flow of water was much greater then, the Hodder not yet tapped by Lancashire's thirsty enterprises.

Today the river can be crossed by way of the hipping stones, but when the river swells this method of crossing can be most perilous and I would strongly advise against it.

Stakes is a large solidly-built dwelling of the Late Stewart period.

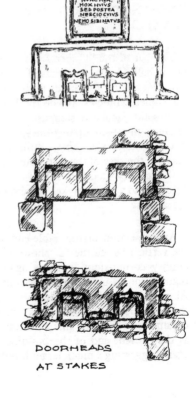

DOORHEADS
AT STAKES

The house is 'T'-shaped and has the strange peculiarity of having two entrance doorways, one to the north, the other to the south, both set in the vertical bar of the 'T'.

Stakes.

Over the north door lintel is a large inscribed stone with the following Latin text: NUNC MEA MOX HUJUS SED POSTEA NEMO SIBI NATUS. A rough translation would be: NOW THIS IS MINE: SOON THIS IS OTHERS: AFTERWARDS WHOSE I KNOW NOT: NOBODY IS BORN FOR HIMSELF.

The bar of the 'T' forms the major part of the hall. On the two ends of each of the two floors are five-light mullioned and transomed windows. Inside the house is a very solid Jacobean staircase and in the kitchen, mounted upon bricks, is a huge circular stone slab-table. Built into the barn, at the rear of the farmhouse, are two 17th century doorheads that may have belonged to a larger Stakes farmhouse than we see now.

An inspection of the gable-end wall of the vertical bar of the 'T' shows irregular clumsy corner-stone work as against the regular quoins used in the horizontal bar. Also notice the hoodmould to the left of the inscribed doorhead. It is what now remains of a window that once ran as far as the present end of the building. Once again suggesting a much larger building.

Stakes Hippings

Stakes was for many years the home of the Astley family, who in the 16th century purchased the manor of Witton in Blackburn, owned before the Dissolution by the monks of Whalley Abbey. The Richmond family followed, and it was they who probably built the present house.

In 1613 there was a Royal Commission concerning a complaint by Henry Richmond of Stakes against Henry Clarke and Thomas Turner. Henry Richmond was tenant by lease from the Crown and the matter in dispute concerned the felling of trees and clearing ground — 'stubbing & grubbing'. We gather that various trees had been removed — oak, ash, birch, alder and willow — and that on the Lees one of the best game coverts had been damaged.

The Toulson family came to Stakes when Clement Toulson married Mary Richmond in c.1660. The fact that a woman became sole heir could explain the uncertainty expressed within the Latin inscription above the north doorway. As to why the owner expressed himself in Latin is open to speculation — possibly he felt that the rustics who could not read Latin need not be catered for, while any gentlemen who came that way would be duly impressed by the learned language on the house.

Stakes to Lower Lees

Walk back up the lane to pass through the gate we came through. Follow right-hand fence and after crossing stream cross the field on a left-diagonal to go over stile. Follow left-hand fence on to enter farm lane and left into Lower Lees.

Lower Lees

The Lees, recorded in the Norman Survey as Sotelie and consisting of three carucates of land, comprises five farmsteads; Higher Lees, Middle Lees, Lower Lees, Lee House and Stakes.

The area covered by the Lees is bisected by the Roman military way which runs from Ribchester over the Bowland Fells to Overborough, and for the greater part of its length the road is still in use today. Given its situation near the watercourse and close proximity to the Roman road, the original Anglo-British settlement was probably near to Middle Lees.

In the early 16th century the Lees was partly wooded, partly marshy tract of land used for rough grazing. From the middle of the 16th century this ground was colonised and steadily enclosed, and the dates of origin of certain farms

can be traced. In 1567
Thomas Turner is
recorded as having
felled timber to
build a house. This
was probably Higher
Lees, occupied in
1652 by his descend-
ant, another Thomas
Turner.

Lower Lees, occupied
in 1652 by Robert
Parker, was built by his father
Alexander Parker in 1596.

The same Alexander Parker
in 1621 is recorded as having
destroyed two acres of woodland. He gave Henry Robinson
enough timber to build a cot-
tage which was occupied by Robinson or his descendant of the same name in
1652. As these new farmsteads were built, so the woodland wastes around
them were gradually cleared.

Near Stakes Farm eight acres of woodland were enclosed in 1603 and a further
three acres in 1621. In 1613 Thomas Turner stubbed (to pull up by the roots)
fourteen acres of woodland, whilst further enclosures were made by the Rathmell family of Lower Lees in 1622 & 1631.

Lower Lees is a plain 17th century farmhouse. The door lintel, with ogee
decoration, is similar to that at Stakes. It bears the date 1678 with the initials
A.R.E., being those of the Rathmell family. Above the ground floor mullioned
windows and the doorway is a continuous string moulding. In the garden are
several old troughs and an ancient grindstone.

Lower Lees to Middle Lees

Walk up the farm lane to fork left, through gateway to Lower Lees Cottage.
Walk around the garden wall to follow left-hand fence on to go through next
gate. Walk on, heading left down the field to go over footbridge. Right, and
walk up to enter Middle Lees by small gate on right of barn.

Middle Lees

Middle Lees is a large substantial house built by the Towneley family during two periods recorded on date shields set into the front gables. In the front garden stands a rather unusually designed sundial, belonging more to the space-age than the 19th century. All nestles in a delightfully laid out garden.

If you wish, you can now return to Whitewell via Radholme Laund to gain one of the most magnificent views to be had of the Hodder Valley as you descend the laund to Whitewell.

Middle Lees to Radholme Laund

Walk down, over the bridge and turn left to pass through a small gate in the wall. Ford the brook and follow it to go over stile in fence. Follow right-hand fence to go through a gate. Walk straight on to ford the brook and on, to go through a gate into farmyard. Walk past the house to go through a gate onto old trackway.

Follow trackway to edge of field and walk on towards lone tree to go over stile by gate. Walk up the field to go over stile in wall in corner of wood. Follow right-hand wall to go over stile and on, following right-hand wall into Radholme Laund farmyard.

Radholme Laund

In the Norman Survey of 1086, Radun was recorded as consisting of two carucates of land being part of the capital manor of Gretlintone (Grindleton). The place-name refers to a settlement of red-haired Norsemen on the flat upland plain above Cow Ark. It is from this spot that travellers through the centuries have gained their spectacular view of the Hodder Valley as they journeyed on towards the Trough and Lancaster.

During the 13th century the conversion of a large part of the Forest of Bowland to vaccaries and pastures hastened its decline as a hunting ground. This led to the creation of a deer park at Radholme. Radholme park lay on a limestone hill rising to over 600 ft. on the east bank of the Hodder, north, south and east of Whitewell.

The boundary, consisting of a ditch and bank, can be reconstructed from field-names and evidence from records of old tenures. It ran east from near the confluence of Withens Brook and the Hodder to Park Gate Farm, then north past Higher Park Gate Farm and over the high ground of Burholme Moor, turning west to join the Hodder below Burholme Farm. The Hodder itself formed the western boundary.

The fences surrounding the park consisted of a ditch of 8 ft. wide and 4½ ft. deep, with the earth thrown up on the outer side to form a bank which was surmounted by a fence of stakes or 'pales' of split oak, on either side of which were three rows of thorns. Gaps in the fences allowed deer to be released into the Forest for hunting as required. The pales were in constant need of renewal and the demand for timber quickly depleted the resources of the park.

Custody of the park was undertaken from a lodge, which was the only habitation in the grounds until the 16th century. This building would have been of a timber construction with a thatched roof. The lodge at Radholme stood on the present site of Radholme Laund.

The park was used exclusively for hunting/breeding for only a short period being gradually transformed later into rented pastures. The cattle enclosures were surrounded by hedged banks lower than those surrounding the park, but high enough to contain the cattle while allowing free passage to the deer.

The leasing of the vaccaries and deer park began the process of the destruction of the game and woodlands of the forest. Although tenants were not allowed to erect fences against the deer and were prohibited from hunting and killing them, the number of deer declined because little attempt was made to enforce the regulations.

Only in the time of the de Lacys was Bowland regarded primarily as a hunting ground. After it had passed to the Earldom and Duchy of Lancaster the new lords showed little interest in the area and rarely hunted there. The deer became the prey of tenants and local gentry and unrestricted poaching whittled away their numbers.

The woodland was similarly destroyed, for the demands made upon it exceeded its power of regeneration. The rate of removal was such that by the early 16th century it was beginning to be in very short supply. It is from this time onwards that we see stone being used as the major building material within the region.

Radholme Laund to Whitewell

Go through a gate on the left of the barn. Follow right-hand wall to go through kissing-gate and through next kissing-gate on the right. Follow left-hand wall to go through a gate and on down following left-hand wall to go over stile in wall on right. Walk straight down, over the lane and on, to go through gateway onto road. Walk down the road to Whitewell.

Middle Lees to Lee House

Walk down over the bridge to go left up the road to go right at bend down the Roman road. Walk on to go through left-hand gate at bottom corner. Cross the field on a left diagonal to cross brook by trees. Walk up the banking and pass through small gate. Walk on to follow left-hand fence to go through gate at edge of pine wood. Walk on to go over footbridge on right. Walk on to go over stile by gate and on to meet with old farm track. Left, and follow track to Lee House.

Lee House

The Jacobean farmhouse of Lee House is hidden away behind a cluster of farm buildings. The frontage displays a fine array of mullioned windows. The doorhead is of a three-arch design with a date tablet above; R.B. 1678.

Lee House to Browsholme Hall

Pass through the gate opposite the large round blue tank to go over stile at rear of new house. Work your way as best you can downstream to ford at meeting of streams. Go through the gate and up the hill to go through gate. Follow right-hand fence to barn. Follow trackway on to go through gate as track curves to the left. Walk on to corner of farmhouse to enter yard by gate. Follow the farm lane for some distance to go through gate on left as the lane curves to the right to meet the roadway. Cross the field on a right-diagonal to go through gate onto road at right of house. Walk on up to Browsholme Lodge.

Browsholme Hall

Home of the Parker family, Browsholme Hall is a superb example of a Jacobean country house. The hall has a symmetrical red sandstone front with two short projecting wings. The centre is taken by a frontpiece of three superimposed orders of Classical couple columns; Doric, Ionic and Corinthian, reminiscent of those at Stonyhurst College.

Inside can be found an Elizabethan overmantel brought from Hapton Tower, and on the first floor is an oak parlour displaying very fine late 17th century woodworking. The Hall houses many treasures and is well worth a visit.

This home of the Parker family, hereditary Bowbearers of the Forest of Bowland, is open to the public every Saturday in June, July and August, and on other dates between April and September by arrangement with Mrs Parker. Tel: Stonyhurst 330.

Browsholme to Crimpton

From the lodge walk a few yards up the lane to go through gate on the left. Follow trackway up, over cattle-grid and through gate opposite. Walk up the field to the right of wood to go over stile by gate. Walk up to go over stile. Walk up to fence and follow it to the right to go over stile at old gate-posts. Cross field on a right diagonal towards the Spire. Enter by stile and follow left-hand fence over stone stile onto farm track. Cross track and walk down to the right of the brick hut to go over stile in fence on right. Follow fence down to go over stiles onto road. Right, then left to go up farm lane to Crimpton.

The Spire

The Spire at Browsholme Heights is a folly built by the Parkers of Browsholme to act as a landmark for shooters on the fells. It consists of a castellated wall with a central Gothic arch, the latter is now bricked up. From a distance it gives the appearance of a church tower.

Crimpton

The lonely fellside farmstead of Crimpton is known locally as 'Our Lady of the Fells'. In the 1500's Crimpton was known as Cromptendenhead after the brook and dene that run down to Birkett. Notice the upper window of seven lights. Handloom weaving was done here in the 18th century, helping to subsidise the meagre hill-farmers' income. A similar set of windows can be found at Batesons (Browsholme Heights) just over the fell.

Crimpton to Whitewell

Go through the gate at the end of the yard and follow left-hand wall/fence past the tree line onto the moor. On a slight left-diagonal head for the inner corner of the pine plantation to go over stile. Follow pine-lined avenue to go over stiles onto hillside.

Walk down to the right of Hell Hole Wood (Hell Hole Pot is a grade III cave. Entry is via a large open shaft situated in a small wood. Keep well away from the mouth of the hole as a fall would be fatal), on down to go over stile by far left tree.

Cross the field and follow the pathway to go through the gate near small wood. Pass through gate on the opposite side of the road. Walk down to the far gateway. Pass through kissing-gate and walk down to Seed Hill Farm. Turn right after the farm and walk down to pass through gateway onto the road above the Whitewell Inn.

The Inn at Whitewell

Walter Urswyck's manor house is now known as The Inn at Whitewell, and some of the early 15th century building remains within the present fabric.

The original manor house was the Swainmote Court; both the Swainmote and Woodmote Courts met here. The forest tenants would come and give accounts of their doings to the Master Forester and his Keepers. The forecourt of the present hotel was once the local market-place for the district.

In 1652, during the Commonwealth, a survey was made of the Chase Of Bowland, and described how the deer park at Radholme was organised at that time. There were officers of the Chase, being twelve Keepers of the Deer, both red and fallow.

The Keeper of the fallow deer was allowed two horses yearly and 'a certain house by the name of Whitewell House or Lodge, in the tenure of Widow Seed, with a barn belonging and a little piece of ground to the west end of the house'.

One of the many good stories told about the Inn is of Peregrine Towneley and his purchase of the Whitewell property. This clever but somewhat erratic old gentleman had always wished to own this property, for the scenery is very delightful. Mr Towneley, with his innate sense of grim humour, loved a joke, and apparently never cared in the least what people thought of him.

THE INN AT WHITEWELL

Hearing that the Whitewell was for sale, he dressed himself as a tramp in old tattered clothes, and, with a clay pipe in his mouth, begged a breakfast at the Whitewell Inn on the day on which the sale by auction was announced. He was given porridge and beans, and when he had finished he strolled into the auction room and enquired what estate was for sale. On being informed that it was the Whitewell estate, he laughed, and said he might as well make a bid for it himself.

The assembled company were highly amused that an old tramp should presume to bid for the extensive property, and told him that they were awaiting the arrival of the 'big man' of the neighbourhood. "And who is your big man?" enquired the tramp. "Why, Peregrine Towneley, of course," was the reply. "He is coming here today, and his price is sure to be far higher than any other, for everyone knows he is very keen on getting this place."

The tramp said that he would begin the bidding while they were waiting, and thereupon named a ridiculously small sum. There were roars of laughter, and someone by way of carrying on the joke bid a little higher. The tramp went higher still, and then the auctioneer, entering into the fun, knocked down the estate to the old tramp for an absurd amount, under the mistaken belief that he could not possibly pay.

He then asked in derision what name was to be entered in his book as the purchaser of the property, whereupon the unknown traveler walked up to the desk and laid a small white card bearing the words 'Mr Peregrine Towneley, Towneley Hall, Burnley' before the horrified auctioneer.

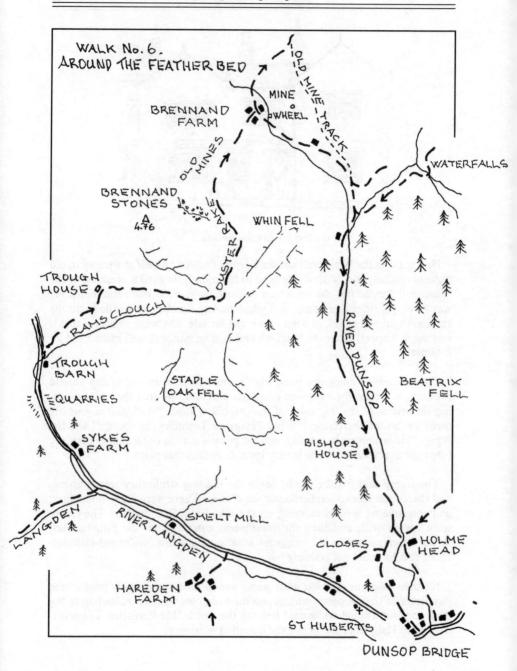

WALK No. 6.
AROUND THE FEATHER BED

OLD MINE TRACK

MINE

WHEEL

BRENNAND
FARM

WATERFALLS

OLD MINES

BRENNAND
STONES
△
476

DUSTER RAKE

WHIN FELL

TROUGH
HOUSE

RAMS CLOUGH

TROUGH
BARN

QUARRIES

STAPLE
OAK FELL

RIVER DUNSOP

BEATRIX
FELL

SYKES
FARM

BISHOPS
HOUSE

LANGDEN

RIVER LANGDEN

SMELT MILL

CLOSES

HOLME
HEAD

HAREDEN
FARM

ST HUBERTS

DUNSOP BRIDGE

Walk 6

AROUND THE FEATHER BED

7 miles, 3½ hours.

MAP: *OS. Sheet SD 65/75, PATHFINDER 660.*

LUNCH: *Flask & Packed Lunch.*

START: *Langden car park, Trough of Bowland.*

This walk can be linked with 'The Kings Silver Mynes in Bolland' walk for a fuller day out. I would suggest you walk over to Whitendale and return to Dunsop via the waterfalls.

This walk takes us from the Trough over to Brennand via Whins Brow. The views gained from the heights are superb — the 'Heart of Bowland' in all its glory and to the north Wolfhole Crag lures, enticing one to wander deeper into the forbidden depths. A rewarding walk, but too short is our pleasure.

Langden Car Park to Sykes Farm

Walk up the road to the farm.

Sykes Farm

In 1322 the family of Adam Langto of Whitendale are recorded as tenants of the vaccary (stock farm) of Glastirdale, now Sykes Farm with Trough Farm. Glastirdale/Lasterdale is now recalled in the river-name Losterdale on whose banks Sykes Farm stands.

By 1407 the Bonde family, relatives of the Langtos, were tenants of Sykes up to a time when in the late 17th century the Parkinson family took over the tenure.

The present owner of Sykes Farm, a strong and sturdy Bolland fellow, informs me that at one time the farmhouse served as a wayside inn for travellers along the Trough road.

SYKES FARM 1692

Over a door of one of the ample barns near the farmhouse are the following letters cut in the hard stone from Birket Quarry on the Knowlmere Estate AIP. TMP. IP. 1692. Down the road, above a cowshed door, can be found another decorated doorhead IAP. TP. 1687.

These initials represent members of the Parkinson family, strict Roman Catholics, who were numerous at that time between here and Bleasdale.

Sykes seems to have been at one time or another a refuge for recusants, and later for the followers of the 1st and 2nd Pretenders. A Mr. Harris was living there in retirement or seclusion on account of his religion and participation in the rising of 1715.

During the last War a Searchlight Unit was based on the flat of land below Sykes, manned by twelve men.

Sykes Mine & Smelt Mill

Beyond Sykes Farm, on either side of Losterdale Brook, are two quarries in the core of the Sykes anticline, a fold running for some miles to the north east; notice that the rock strata in this part of the Trough are steeply tilted and in places very much bent. In the quarry on the east of the road the folding and contortions in the strata are very well displayed.

Inspection of the rocks in the quarries reveals that the strata are badly broken and that there is a good deal of vein breccia among them — mainly a poor quality vein stuff with barite, both pink and white, with a little quartz as the commonest mineral. There is also some fluor spar, fragments of galena, calamine and some staining by copper minerals.

In the 19th century a small mine worked three veins in the west quarry and the position of the mines can still be made out. A series of small openings can be seen near the top of the quarry face; all these lead into small irregular and ramified workings, with no proper mine passages. Such ore that was won occurred in small bunches and flots. There is no record of production but it could never have been much.

Below Sykes Farm, by the cattle-grid, stand Smelt Mill Cottages at the foot of Smelt Mill Clough. The cottages stand by the low remains of the smelt mill that once served both the Skyes and Brennand mines, the Brennand ore being transported over the hill by way of Ouster Rake track.

Today the 'Smelt Mill' is the Headquarters of the Bowland Pennine Mountain Rescue Team — a hard working group who deserve every support.

Sykes Farm to Brennand Farm

Follow the road on, passing Sykes Quarries to pass through gate at Trough Barn. Follow the track up to the ruin of Trough House. Pass through gate and follow track on up Bleashaw Clough and over the moor to go over ladder-stile. Follow path on up and around to the left to post and on to go over fence-stile.

Follow path on (good view over Middle Knoll) beneath the Brennand Stones to go through gate. Follow the Ouster Rake path on down, over fence-stile and on to pass through gateway and over stile into Brennand farmyard.

Brennand to Langden Car Park

Follow the roadway down, past Foot Holme Water Works, and on down, past Bishop's House to the cattle-grid at Closes Farm. Walk to the rear of the house to go over wall by iron gates and on, following left-hand wall to corner above barns.

Walk over to the right to pass through gate onto road. Follow the road on, past the Smelt Mill (Bowland Pennine Mountain Rescue Team) to the Langden Car Park.

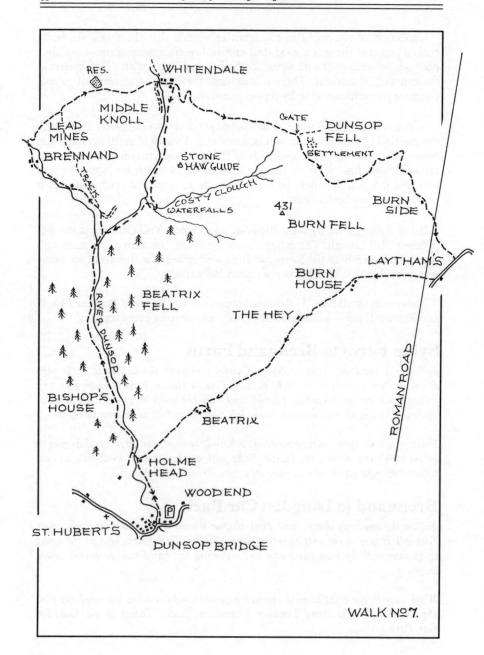

RES.

WHITENDALE

MIDDLE
KNOLL

LEAD
MINES

GATE

DUNSOP
FELL

BRENNAND

STONE
HAW GUIDE

SETTLEMENT

TRACK

COSTY CLOUGH

WATERFALLS

431

BURN FELL

BURN
SIDE

LAYTHAM'S

BURN
HOUSE

BEATRIX
FELL

THE HEY

RIVER DUNSOP

BISHOP'S
HOUSE

BEATRIX

ROMAN ROAD

HOLME
HEAD

WOODEND

ST. HUBERT'S

P

DUNSOP BRIDGE

WALK Nº 7.

Walk 7

'THE KINGS SILVER MYNES IN BOLLAND'

(The Brennand, Dunsop Head, Beatrix Round)

10½ miles, 5 hours. The full round.
7½ miles, 3 hours. Brennand, Whitendale round.

MAP: *O.S. sheet 65/75, PATHFINDER 660.*

LUNCH: *Flask & Packed Lunch*

START: *Dunsop Bridge car park (Toilets/Post Office shop/Petrol).*

This walk is a well loved favourite with upland walkers who appreciate the wild moorland tops and rugged valley bottoms. It should not be attempted in bad weather as one could get lost in the deep peat hags around Dunsop Head. Keep to the waymarked track (yellow tipped poles) and do not stray. I also advise you to stay clear of the lead mine shafts and openings as these can be very dangerous places indeed. The props holding the roof timbers are old and rotten.

Use common sense and have a great day's walking, enjoying scenic views over the Hodder Valley and Craven which are second to none.

Dunsop Bridge Car Park to Brennand Farm

Walk down to the Post Office to take the trackway on the right just below the bridge and follow it on to the rear of Holme Head Cottages. Pass over stile and walk on to go over footbridge. Follow the Brennand road up the valley, past the Water Works and on to the junction with the Whitendale road.

Follow road to the left (the gateway up on the right opens onto an old miners trackway that some walkers use to gain long views over the Brennand valley en-route for the Middle Knoll saddle) to Brennand Farm.

Brennand

Brennand Farm stands in the remote, wild and infertile north-west of Bowland, an ancient vaccary established by the monks of Whalley Abbey.

In the late 17th century the farmhouses at Brennand and Whitendale were primitive cruck-framed structures open to the roof divided into two or three rooms — little different from those of their mediaeval predecessors. The barns, again cruck-framed, are described in 1652 as 'large open church-like structures . . . made of large baulks of timber, entire oak trees, springing from a low wall and meeting in the centre in a pointed arch'. The roofs would have been thatched. This type of construction gave way to the buildings of stone that we see today.

Tradition holds that there was once a chapel at Brennand, mentioned by Abbot Lindley of Whalley in c.1347. The monks of Whalley then wrote: 'It should be remembered that there was once in Bouland a certain chapel called Brennand chapel, which chapel then belonged to the parish church of Whalley.'

Supporting this tradition is a stone marked with the Christian monogram IHS and five crosses that once stood by the farmhouse door at Brennand. Today the stone is built into the altar in the chapel at Whalley Abbey

Conference House and known as the
'Brennand Stone'.

Upon examination of the stone at
Whalley, I personally consider it to
be a portable altar stone. This type of
stone could he carried in a saddle
bag, thus enabling the lord and his
retainers to hear the Mass even when
on hunting trips in the Forest of
Bowland performed by an accom-
panying priest.

Standing near to the farmhouse
at Brennand is an old mahogany
panelled grouse keepers' cabin. During the breeding season a keeper had to
spend some time on the fells looking after the birds. At such times the wheeled
cabin would be provisioned and horse-drawn onto the fells, providing the
keeper with a mobile living place. During the game season it also served as a
shooters' refreshment cabin.

The place-name 'Brennand' is an intriguing one, derived from Old Norse
'the burning one'. It may refer to the red hair of some Northman, or, as some
think, to the 'Middle Knoll Phenomenon'. This occurs during late May and
early June when the sun makes its setting over Morecambe Bay, a minute after
total sunset in the Hodder Valley a shaft of the sun's final rays strikes through
one of the many ravines which bisect the Bowland fells. The light appears
to run up Middle Knoll like a forest fire until the whole west side is il-
luminated. A few moments later the phenomenon retreats and dusk takes over
the twilight. The 'Burning One' is best viewed from the summit of New
Laund Hill above the Whitewell Gorge.

West of Brennand, resting high in the ling below Ughtersik (Millers House)
is Brennand Tarn. The brakish waters are said to hold the gold and silver plate
brought from Whalley Abbey during the Dissolution for hiding. Sadly, for
those seeking quick fortune and wealth, there is no foundation whatsoever for
this story; the Whalley plate was all accounted for by Henry VIII's commis-
sioners.

Below the farmstead, set into the opposite bank of the river, are the remains
of a water-wheel pit — part of a once lead mining enterprise.

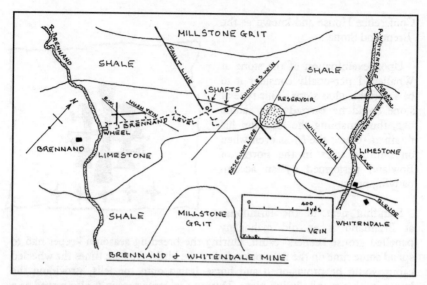

Brennand Mine

The Brennand Mine covers an area of ground between the Brennand and Whitendale valleys occupied by the core of the Sykes anticline (the arch in a fold of rock strata) that has formed a short cross valley between two approximately oval areas of limestones. The exposed limestone cores of the anticlines are surrounded by shales with ironstone and thin limestone bands.

These are framed in Pendle Grits of Millstone Grit age, which completely surround them. The limestone and lower shales are crossed by a number of short faults, most of them across the axis of the fold. Some of these faults have been mineralized, the major minerals being galena and barite, with some fluor spar and a little blende and calamine.

The earliest evidence for mining in the Brennand area has been noted west of Brennand Farm around Swine Clough. Scattered about here are lumps of galena and occasionally blende, remnants of early working, pre 17th century.

The Brennand and Brunghill mines, part of 'The Kinges Silver Mynes in Bowland', were first worked in 1610 by Sir Belvis Bulmer who 'brought the mine to great perfection, and getting great store of Silver Ore.'

Sir Belvis was the first Englishman to gain a reputation as a mining engineer. He came to prominence in 1586 in the Mendip mines, and in 1587 was in charge of mining and smelting at the king's mines at Combe Martin, Devon. In 1597 he had a partnership with Thomas Foullis in lead and silver mines in Scotland; he died on Alston Moor in 1615.

The rich silver ore won from the Bowland mines was most likely to be an oxidation zone concentration near the surface and of limited occurrence, not at all likely to be sustained in deeper workings.

Bulmer's Essay Master at the Brennand mines was one Walter Basby. After Bulmer's death Basby "was sent to the Emperor of Russia to settle the standard of his coin: where he remained diverse years, and going down to the borders of Tartaria to view the mines there, was taken prisoner by the Tartars, and after redeemed by the Russian Emperor and sent over to England.

"Where after about the year 1655 he was again brought down (to Bowland) with some Londoners" (quotes from 'Mettalographia: or an History of Metals' by John Webster. London MDCLXXI).

BRENNAND MINE

Basby and his Londoners made several trials but failed to recover any good quantity of silver, and that gained, not the best ore.

The mines were worked off and on up to 1874, then being deemed worked out, leaving the few remains that we see today. These include the reservoir that was formed on the ground just above the shaft head to supply power for a water-wheel for both winding and dressing of which only traces of this wheel-pit now remain.

There was another water-wheel at the mouth of the adit, on the river bank below Brennand Farm, of which only an eroded structure remains. This wheel powered a crusher and a dressing floor. The smelt mill was located below Sykes on the Trough road, ore being carried over from Brennand via the Ouster Rake track with little difficulty.

The Whitendale side of the hill is marked with many ancient and overgrown bell-pit workings, with no trace whatever of an adit or opencast work. These could be the traces of the 17th century workings.

Brennand to Whitendale

Pass through farmyard and on down to go over the bridge. Follow the trackway on the right up, over stile by gate and on up and around to the left to go over stile by gate. Follow wall on to go over stile and on past the reservoir to follow path on and down, through wall-gate and on down to Whitendale via bridge.

Whitendale

Whitendale — 'the dale of the white ling (heather)', is a very well tended remote Bowland farmstead. The main farmstead was built by the Towneley family in 1854 — recorded on a stone above the doorway. The keeper's cottage still has a mullion sill and topstone, pointing to a 17th century origin.

The shorter walk now returns to Dunsop Bridge.

Whitendale to Dunsop Bridge

Pass through the farmyard and follow the wall around to the right to pick up a pathway. Walk on, through gate and on to go over stream and through next gate. Walk on to pass through gate (notice the B.C.W.W. iron markers of the former Blackburn Corporation Water Works) and on to the waterfalls. Follow path on and down the zig-zags to follow the stream down to Dunsop track.

Whitendale to Dunsop Head Gate

Pass through the farmyard and follow the track that zig-zags up the hillside to follow stake-marked pathway up and on to the gate in wall at Dunsop Head. Pass through the gate.

Dunsop Head

The positioning of some of the scattered gritstones here suggests the hand of man at work. A recent survey has placed a Bronze Age provenance on the site though no artifacts have been found.

Dunsop Head to Laythams

Follow the line of the wall to the right for some way to work your way around the steep clough to find a well-defined trackway. Follow the track around Burn Fell End down to Burn Side Farm. Pass over stiles and follow the farm lane down to the roadway. Right, and walk down to Laythams.

Laythams

The Roman Road between Ribchester and Over Burrow (CALACVM) crosses the fields to the west of the farm, and in the field to the north of Laythams are some curious ditch and bank earthworks.

Laythams to Beatrix

Go through the gate opposite Laythams and cross the field on a left diagonal to go over fence-stile. Walk on, keeping on the same line, over stream and on keeping well to the right of the old air raid shelter to go over wall-stile and on to far corner of field. Follow the trackway through 17th century Burn House and on past the Hey to go over cattle-grid. Walk on to go through gate on right of stone post. Follow left-hand hedgerow to go through gate on right. Follow clough down to go through small gate at bottom. Cross the stream and go directly up to follow ditch across the field to pass through gateway. Cross the field on a left diagonal to go through gateway. Follow right-hand fence down and round to the left to enter Beatrix farmyard.

Beatrix to Dunsop Bridge

Follow the farm lane round, past the lower barns and house to go over into the field on the right. Follow overhead cables across the field to go over stile into wood. Walk down the banking to go over fence-stile. Left, and enter Holme Head via small gate. Follow the lane down to Dunsop Bridge.

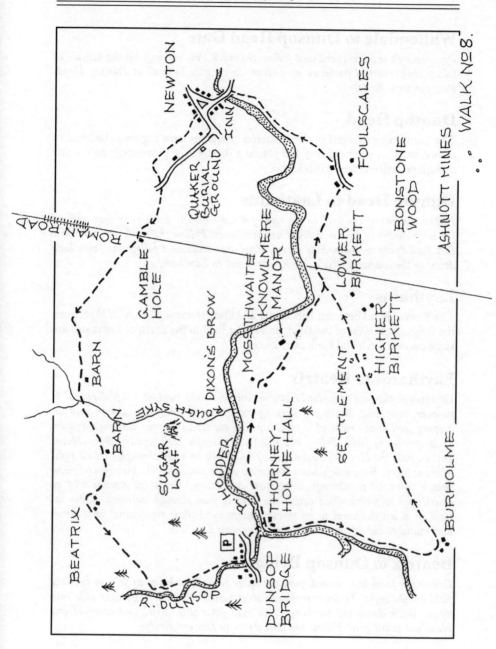

Walk 8

HILL FARMS OF THE NORTHMEN

8 miles, via Burholme.
6½ miles via Mossthwaite. 5 or 4 hours.

MAP: *O.S. SD 64/74 & 65/75 PATHFINDER SERIES.*

LUNCH: *Parkers Arms, Newton.*

START: *Dunsop Bridge Car Park*
             (Toilets at Dunsop & Newton).

In this walk we go above the River Hodder to explore a number of ancient settlements and changing landscapes. The uplands between Dunsop and Newton truly belong to a former age, a 'lost world' known only to the few who have ventured into these sheltered vale-cut plateaus. The farmsteads visited hold some surprising stories and historical remains. A shorter walk can be made by way of Mossthwaite.

Dunsop Bridge

The village of Dunsop stands at the foot of the 'Feather Bed' (watershed), the old name for the Trough of Bowland, that climbing moorland track to Lancaster which is the haunt of walker and motorist alike. Sited in the heart of the Duchy of Lancaster Estates in Lancashire the surrounding area is home to large flocks of sheep, cattle, grouse and deer. On a fine day the riverside attracts many visitors, being a favourite picnic spot. A good place to find contentment and let your thoughts float downstream and the world pass by.

Dunsop grew up around a blacksmith's forge, now the local garage. The original village site is to be found at Beatrix, now a single farmstead but once a thriving hamlet with regular markets which traded from the 13th until the 18th century.

DUNSOP BRIDGE

The place-name Beatrix comes from the ancient Hiberno-Norse settlement of 'Bothvar's Ergh' which was established during the 10th century. In those times these Hiberno-Norse Vikings settled and farmed the marginal lands on the borders of the Northern Hundreds/Shires (these borders follow those of the older Celtic Cantrevs of the North), in this case Blackburnshire and Cravenshire.

At Mill House in Dunsop stands a roughly carved-out stone, mounted and now serving as a bird bath. This is said to be an old holy-water font found on the site of the old chapel at Burholme Farm.

For many years the font rested in the Dames School at the now Bridge End Cottages in the 1880's. The school was run by the Sisters of Notre Dame who then resided at the Towneley houses of Staple Oak and Thorneyholme. The 'font' is more likely to have served as a holy-water stoop if it did come from a chapel.

In the garden of one of the cottages at Dunsop sits an ancient stone mortar which was found in the river — a lost household utensil of some early valley inhabitants.

To the south west of the village stands Mellor Knoll, known affectionately by locals as 'The Old Man of Bol-

QUERN
STONE
DUNSOP BR.

land'. When viewed beyond Thorneyholme, en-route for Burholme, the hill has the appearance of a rotund gentleman sleeping the afternoon away after a dinner-time session in the Whitewell. During the summer months the leafy foliage on the north end give the Old Man a fine crop of curly hair. The name Mellor is of Celtic (British) origin, and means 'bare hill'.

The shorter walk to Foulscales, by way of Mossthwaite, is described first, along with a description of Knowlmere Manor.

Dunsop Bridge Car Park to Foulscales via Knowlmere

Come out of the car park to follow the road to the left to enter the Redwood driveway of Thorneyholme Hall. Walk on to pass over the bridge and go through gate on the left onto riverbank pathway. Walk on, through gate and follow fence on to go over stile. Follow line of fence to the right to cross stream. Cross the field on a right diagonal to pass through gate in wall.

Follow trackway to the left, through gate and on to enter Mossthwaite via gate. Follow estate road on, passing Knowlmere Manor, to cross Giddy Bridge. Follow estate road on to go left at junction and on to meet the roadway. Walk down the road to view Foulscales over on the right.

Knowlmere Manor

In 1258 the manor of Knowlmere was part of the holdings in Newton of Elias de Knoll. When his grandson, Rayner, Lord of Hellifield, died without issue, Rayner's younger brother, Elias, came into succession.

He died leaving an only daughter, Katherine; she married Adam de Hammerton and brought Hellifield Peel and Knowlmere to that family.

Knowlmere Manor

VINESCROLL

GREEK KEY

INTERLACING

When Sir Stephen Hammerton forfeited his estates for his part in the Pilgrimage of Grace, Knowlmere was sold to Robert Parker, in whose family it remained for many generations.

The manor was later granted by the Crown to Cuthbert Musgrave. It is now owned by the Peel family who purchased it from the Duke of Buccleuch. The Peels of Knowlmere are related to the Peels of Blackburn, descendants of Sir Robert Peel. The family grave stands in the grounds of Blackburn Cathedral.

Alice Peel of Knowlmere was a keen local historian and produced several good books on the Bowland area, one of which was a short illustrated history entitled 'The Manor of Knowlmere' (Preston, 1913). From her description of the manor in the 16th century, it would appear that the place was almost a small village in those days.

The present house is built in the Gothic Revival style of the late Victorian era: with its many gables and chimneys it presents an interesting picture. The parkland adjoining the Manor is exceptionally well maintained and their fine condition is most pleasing to the eye.

Stored at the Knowlmere Estate is a shaft fragment of an ancient cross. Known as 'Oldhams Cross', it was brought by the Peels from their house at Peel Fold, Blackburn in the 19th century.

Peel Fold was originally called Oldham Cross, after an Oswaldtwistle family that lived there in the 16th century and the cross that stood nearby. I, like many others, would dearly like to see this cross returned to the Parish of Blackburn.

The shaft is of pre-Conquest date with a vine-scroll design on its two main faces. The sides bear an interlaced design and Greek Key pattern respectively. The workmanship is Hiberno-Norse influenced of a 10th/11th century date.

Dunsop Bridge to Burholme

Walk down the Redwood-lined Thorneyholme driveway, over the bridge to go right, into the yard and through the gate. Follow the riverside pathway over three stiles to cross a field and pass through gateway. Walk up the rise, bearing left to enter Burholme by gate near stream and on to front of house.

Burholme

Although only a single farmstead today, Burholme was once a small hamlet and may even be the 'lost' Domesday vill recorded then as 'Bogewrde' — the first element being 'bow' (bend in a river as in Bowland), the second being 'wearda', Old Norse 'voroa', meaning beacon or cairn.

The site of the cairn or beacon could have been Kitcham Hill, possibly a former Roman signal station given its close proximity to the Roman Road between Ribchester and Overbrough.

BURHOLME

Some time in the 14th century the village and church at Burholme were abandoned and the inhabitants moved to Whitewell (c.1400) when the Radholme Deer Park was established. The richly carved font from Burholme Chapel is now in use as a Holy Water stoop at St Hubert's Church, Dunsop.

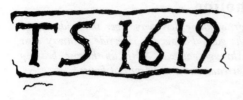

With the decline of the Deer Park, Burholme re-established itself as a small hamlet. The 1527 Rent Roll records at least six families living here. The old village is now the site of an archaeological investigation by the Pendle Heritage Archaeological Group. The positions of at least eight 16th century buildings have been identified and two have been excavated along with a circular structure of unknown provenance.

Before 1590, the dwelling houses were of wood and thatch, often comprising only one room. By the mid-17th century wood had given way to stone and only the poorest families still dwelt in these primitive cruck-framed houses. However, rebuilding in stone was slow to spread to outbuildings — all barns recorded in Bowland for 1652 were of the timber, cruck-framed type.

The farmhouse today at Burholme incorporates two early 17th century buildings and was refronted in the early 19th century. Notice the huge gable chimney stack.

The barn is dated 1619 with the initials of Thomas Swinhulhurst, and below this datestone the following is inscribed: I JANE LOVE FOR TRU TO W*** AND FAITHFUL I WILL BE. Other carved stones to be found on the building, known as 'Quaker Stones', bear much faded inscriptions and dates of c.1735.

These stones record Quaker emigrations to Pennsylvania, founded by William Penn in 1682, in the 18th century. These Pilgrims built a town there and named it Burholme and each year many of their descendants return to view their ancestral Bowland homeland.

The higher barn at Burholme is also of great interest. The timbers of the cow stalls come from old dismantled ships, brought down through the Trough of Bowland from Glasson Dock in the 18th century. Behind this barn the old village well stands in a small enclosure. Though now dry it was once fed from natural springs.

Burholme to Foulscales

Walk back to the ford and cross the footbridge to go over stile on right. Follow Fielding Clough up, over stile and on up to pass over next stile. Now follow right-hand wall to where it bends to the right and keep walking directly on, passing Bronze Age site, to the left of the wood on the right to go over wall-stile by gated gap in wall. Walk down on a right diagonal to go over fence-stile and on to go over next stile. Walk on to pass through gate and on to cross Giddy Bridge. Follow lane on the left down to the roadway. Left, and Foulscales is over on the right.

Hodder Bank Fell Ancient Site

Above Higher Birkett, on the summit of Hodder Bank Fell are a number of circular groups of large stones and several chambered cairns. These cairns and stone features were first recorded in 1955, and thought to be of Bronze Age origin.

During the early spring of 1988 the heather and grasses were burned on this part of the fell enabling one to see clearly these normally obscured features. Upon inspecting the site we discovered a central burial cist of large stones surrounded by an outer bank, and a saddle quern half buried nearby leading us to think upon the same lines as the 1955 survey.

Foulscales

Here we find another Old Norse name, meaning foal or fodder shed, and strangely enough it in someway applies to the late 16th century building that we see here today. We have here, in effect, two buildings in one.

The original building was a bastel type dwelling (a 'fortified' dwelling where the main living quarters occupy the first floor) entered by outside stone steps to the first floor. Notice the upper low mullioned windows and the mediaeval latrine (garderobe) set on corbles on the west end of the house. The ground floor would have held both stock and fodder — providing a form of heating to the first floor.

The building underwent a change of usage some time during the 17th century, judging by the size of the ground floor arrangement of mullioned windows. At this time the ground floor was converted for human usage.

During the 16th century, a branch of the Parker family of Browsholme lived at Foulscales and were builders of the present house here.

The Foulscales Stone

This strange stone, anciently known as the Yolstone and later as Bonstone, once stood behind Foulscales, near Gibbs. The stone displays possible early native chi-rho symbols and some later 16/17th century lettering — H T — referring to a member of the Tempest family, then landowners in these parts. Given the design and workmanship, the stone may have a Celtic 6/7th century provenance.

For some reason this stone was removed from its site at Foulscales and taken into the cellars at Knowlmere Manor under the authority of the Peel Estate.

Foulscales to Newton

Walk along the road and after passing the barn with cottage attached go over stile on left. Cross the field on a right-diagonal to pass through gateway and on to go through next gateway and down to the river. Follow fence on to go over stile and follow river on up to go over next stile. Cross the field directly to Newton Bridge, then walk on up into the village.

Newton

'Newtone', recorded on the Norman Survey as part of the manor of Gretlintone (Grindleton), consisted then of four carcurates of land. The ancient town field doles can still be made out in the field to the north west of the village.

The village today has many fine 17th to 19th

century buildings, some with dated Yorkshire lintels displaying fine ornamental workmanship. Those featured here belong to a cottage built by the Slinger family of Newton.

The Parkers Arms is a splendid Georgian building displaying a central stepped Venetian window. The inn has a very good restaurant and bar meals are served daily. Newton Hall, across the way, is a fine Georgian edifice worthy of note, and both buildings present a wonderful frontage to the village when entering by way of Newton Bridge.

SALISBURY COTTAGE

Standing in the centre of the village is Salisbury Hall. Formerly Newton Old Hall, this was once the home of the Salisbury family who are mentioned as lawyers in Slaidburn in 1729. The red sandstone building to the left of the Old Hall was once the lawyer's offices. Notice the two doorways — one was for the lawyer and one for his clerk. A walled-in square field near the river between Newton Bridge and the Roman Bargh Ford is still known as Salisbury Flatts. The Salisburys left Newton in 1750 to live in Lancaster.

On the main street stands John Brabbin's Old School House. It is a bland, flat-fronted house with a date tablet over the door: J.M.B. 1757. Brabbin, in his will of 1768, left twenty guineas to endow a school to be held in this building 'for instructing all people called Quakers and six of the children of the poor not being Quakers.' As a boy in the 1820's, John Bright, a leading light in the Quaker movement, spent two years at the Newton school, and held many fond memories of the place, as he mentioned in his letters later in life.

On a steep pitch above the school is the Friends Meeting House with cottage attached for the caretaker. The house is a two-storey building with a datestone,

1767. A few yards higher up on the far side of the road is a walled enclosure with a locked door, the graveyard of the Quaker community.

The Quaker movement was established in Newton by William Dewsbury, an adherent of George Fox, in 1670. He faired less well in Slaidburn where the villagers set upon him and drove him away. In Settle, Dewsbury was beaten unconscious by an angry mob and was left to lie in the gutter. Having recovered, this man of strong conviction, pursued his grand design only to spend nineteen years in Warwick Gaol for his teachings and beliefs.

The ancient quern stones, pictured here, were found by villagers in the river. They now serve as garden ornaments. These would once have been used for grinding grains, and possibly date back to the Roman period.

ANCIENT QUERN STONES, NEWTON

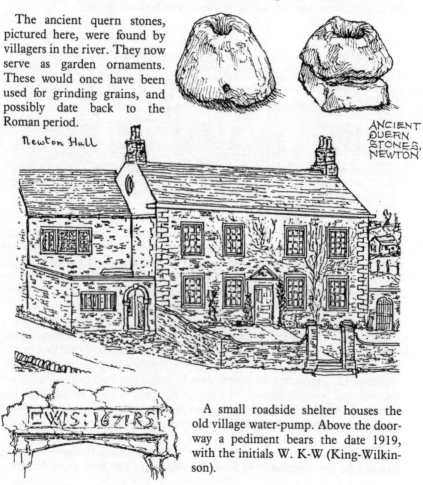

Newton Hall

A small roadside shelter houses the old village water-pump. Above the doorway a pediment bears the date 1919, with the initials W. K-W (King-Wilkinson).

Newton to Gamble Hole Farm

Walk up the farm track behind the village Telephone Box to go over wall-stile on the left of a barn. Walk up the field to pass through gate-stile. Cross the field to corner of wall and on through gate to follow left-hand hedgerow up and round to go down to cross slab-bridge. Walk on up to go over wall-stile onto roadway. Pass through concealed gateway opposite and cross the field on a left diagonal to pass through gateway. Follow hedge-side track to Gamble Role Farm.

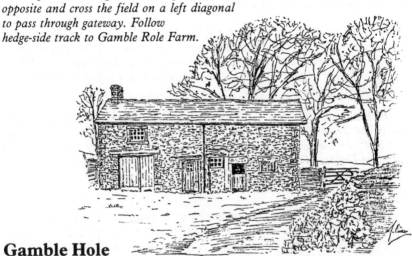

Gamble Hole

This is a strange name for a farmstead and many have thought that it refers to a large deep hole in the field adjoining the barn. This great depression is the remains of an underground chamber whose roof has fallen in, forming a natural quarry for the extraction of limestone. An old lime Kiln can be seen in the banking above the quarry. The whole area, especially the field above Gamble Hole, is dotted with limestone shake-holes — most perilous if the underground roof falls in when one is walking the field above — hence the gamble it is said. However, although this is a colourful theory it is far from correct.

In 1232, Gamble Hole was then recorded as 'Gammellearges'. The first element of the place-name is 'Gamel', an old West Scandinavian personal name. The second is 'argh', meaning a 'shieling' a 'hill pasture' or 'hut on pasture', and is from the Old Norse word 'airge' — cattle/dairy pasture. This gives us a clue to one of the staples of the Bowland economy in the 10th and 11th centuries when the area was settled by Hiberno-Norse peoples from across the Irish Sea.

Foil to The Crag Coiners

Robert Parker was born at Gamble Hole Farm in 1731, sixth child and third son of George Parker, yeoman farmer. Robert's father died in 1736, and a year later his mother married John Dixon, a school master. In 1752, the youngest three children — Henry, Robert and Margaret — with their mother and step-father, moved to Midgley, a tiny hamlet near Halifax. The elder son and two daughters stayed on at Gamble Hole.

Robert later went to study Law at Lincolns Inn, London. In 1753 he was admitted an attorney of the Court of Kings Bench. Late in 1753 he returned to Halifax and joined a law partnership. By 1768 he was Chief Lawyer in Halifax and went on to be the major force in the breaking of the infamous Heptonstall Crag Coiners Gang.

The leader of the 'Crag Coiners' was David Hartley, known around Heptonstall as 'King David'. The two 'hit men' of the gang were Robert Thomas and Matthew Normington, and it was these two who in 1769 killed an excise man near Halifax. Tried at York in 1770, they were discharged on the grounds of lack of evidence — people were afraid of the gang and would not speak out against them.

Robert Parker collected new evidence on the two, but as one could not be tried twice for the same offence, he brought forward a charge against them of highway robbery. Thomas was tried at York on Saturday 16th July, 1774, and was hanged at Tyburn (now York race course) on 6th August, 1774. Normington was given bail, due to lack of evidence. The body of Thomas was hung in chains on Beacon Hill above Halifax. Normington was was again arrested in the spring of 1775, and this time he was found guilty. He was executed at York and hung in chains next to the bird-eaten remains of Thomas.

David Hartley and one of his henchmen, James Oldfield, were found guilty of their crimes and hanged at York on the 28th April, 1770. Because of the work of Robert Parker and William Deighton, the murdered excise man, the Crag Coiners were broken. The state was moved into action, and coins of a standard weight with milled edges were introduced, so protecting against the debasement of the coinage. A book on the subject, 'Clip a Bright Guinea' by John Marsh (Robert Hale Ltd, London 1971) is well worth a read.

Some foolish people around Halifax and Heptonstall have tried to make the gang into folk heroes, but a more nasty group of Yorkshire thugs you would be hard pressed to find.

Gamble Hole Farm has a datestone with the inscription: W.W.1845. The farm across the way, Brown Hills, is dated 1816, with the inscription: Robert & Alice Parker (of) Bury, Lancashire.

Gamble Hole to Beatrix

Pass through the gate on the right of the barn and cross the field on a slight left-diagonal to go through gate onto a trackway. Follow the trackway up and around to go through gate. Follow trackway down, past Rough Syke Barn, down to the stream (to the south, above the stream, stands Sugar Loaf Hill). Cross the stream and pass through the left-hand gate to pass over another stream. Walk up the hill, through two fields to the right of Back-of-the-Hill Barn. Walk on over the hill to enter Beatrix via gate.

Sugar Loaf Hill

Looking south from Rough Syke one sees the pointed limestone hill known locally as the Knot or Sugar Loaf. Viewed from the south one can see that the reef knoll has been quarried and a lime kiln is sited below the workings. On this curious outcrop stood formerly a gibbet, the chains from which were found in a hedgerow nearby.

The area below the Knot is said to be haunted by a boggart, often sighted on the parapet of Rough Syke Bridge.

Beatrix

The hillside farmstead of Beatrix takes its name from the ancient Norwegian farming settlement of Batherarges (Bothvar's Ergh), a hill farm belonging to Bothvar. Hiberno-Norse place-names occur most frequently on the edges of the former Celtic Cantrevs of Northern Britain. In this case north of the Ribble on the edge of the former Blackburnshire.

During the 9th and 10th centuries the Norwegians held all the land which is now contained within the present boundaries of Lancashire and Cumbria. The Danes held Yorkshire. These colonists were Hiberno-Norse Vikings who came over from the Norwegian kingdom of Dublin. Their presence posed a great threat to the rule of the central and southern English kingdoms of

Alfred, Edward the Elder and, later, Athelstan. The latter finally succeeded in the subjection of the North, a conquest which culminated with the Battle of Brunanburh in 937, and the retreat of Anlaf's Viking army, who fled to their ships moored on the River Wyre and returned to Dublin.

The fact that certain Norse place-names survived within the area shows that the influence and people lived on in the marginal lands which surrounded the earlier established Anglo-British settlements.

Beatrix has been an important stock-rearing centre since the early 13th century, and markets were held here in the 17th and 18th centuries. In 1765, Beatrix is recorded as being a hamlet of six holdings with three other holdings which lay on the edge of the old vaccary land. One of the latter has grown from a simple smithy's forge into the modern village of Dunsop Bridge. The other two holdings, Holme Head and Wood End, have changed little from their original size.

Remains of the old village of Beatrix are few, but the careful eye will pick out 17th century doorheads and window mullions built into the fabric of the surrounding farm walls. On the ground between the present two dwellings you can see the grassed-over foundations of the earlier homesteads of long gone villagers.

The lower dwelling at Beatrix has recently been restored into use and is a good example of farm building c.1750. Notice the figure of a sheep set in a niche above the porch doorway. A similar stone carving can be found above the doorway at Wood End.

Beatrix to Dunsop

Follow the farm lane round to pass the lower barns and walk into the field on the right to follow the overhead cables across the field to enter wood via stile. Walk down the banking to go over fence-stile. Left, and enter the rear of Holme Head via gate. Follow lane down to Dunsop.

St. Hubert R.C. Church

Just outside the village, along the Trough road, stands the Roman Catholic Church of St. Hubert, patron saint of foresters. The chapel was built in 1864, and paid for by Richard Eastwood Esq., estate agent to the Towneley family and a resident at Thorneyholme.

The chapel consists of nave and chancel together, apse and bell-cote. The west window and apse have stained glass by Capronnier, dated 1865. Within and outside the chapel many memorials to the Towneley family can be found. Notice the alter side pillars, decorated with four small horses heads.

These represent Kettledrum who won much wealth for the Towneley stables, culminating in the winning of the Derby in the 1880's. In the picturesque grounds stands a huge white marble angel, a memorial to Richard Henry Towneley.

By far the most interesting and intriguing item in the chapel is the Burholme Font, a strangely carved piece of mediaeval art that hints at a far older religious site in Bowland.

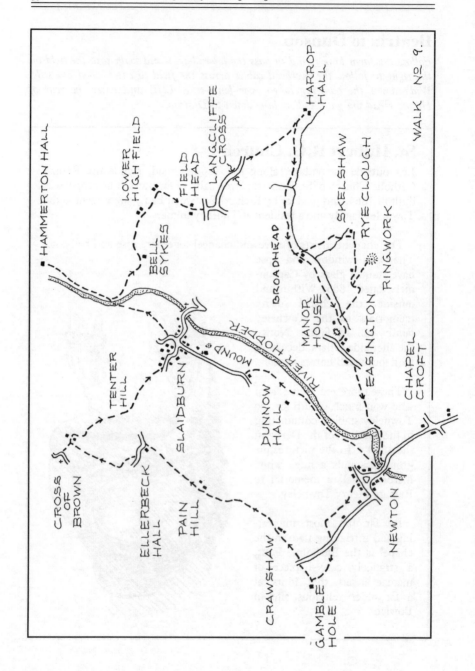

WALK Nº 9.

HARROP HALL

HAMMERTON HALL

LOWER HIGH FIELD

FIELD HEAD

LANGCLIFFE CROSS

SKELSHAW

RYE CLOUGH

BELL SYKES

BROADHEAD

RINGWORK

MANOR HOUSE

EASINGTON

CHAPEL CROFT

MOUND

RIVER HOPPER

TENTER HILL

SLAIDBURN

DUNNOW HALL

CROSS OF BROWN

ELLERBECK HALL

PAIN HILL

NEWTON

CRAWSHAW

GAMBLE HOLE

Walk 9

BY WAY OF KIRKSTALL'S SHEEP FARMS

6 or 8 miles, 3 or 4 hours.

MAP: *O.S. Sheet SD 65/75, PATHFINDER 660.*

LUNCH: *Hark to Bounty, Slaidburn,*
or Parkers Arms, Newton.

START: *Slaidburn riverside car park or Newton.*

Even for those who think they know the Newton and Slaidburn district well this walk will prove to be one of new discoveries. The farmsteads visited are steeped in history so deep that I can only hope to scratch the surface with my present scribblings. Upon each visit I discover some new facet that I have previously overlooked be it a Bronze Age site or carved datestone, nothing would now surprise me. Add to this the terrific local scenery and I am sure that your wanderings will be just as richly rewarding as mine have been.

The longer Ellerbeck walk can be shortened by way of Dunnow Hall from Newton village.

Slaidburn

At the time of the Domesday Survey Slaidburn was part of the manor of Grindleton, but in 1250 the De Lacy lordship discarded Grindleton as head of the manor in favour of Slaidburn.

This ancient sheep farming settlement sits above the Hodder on the banks of Croasdale Brook. Markets were once held at the top of Church Street by the old village cross, the base of which is now built into the side of New Hodder Bridge. Stock and cattle fairs have been held in the village since 1294, and in the 17th century cattle fairs were held four times a year.

The village once had a smithy, a wheelwright, a tannery and a corn mill.

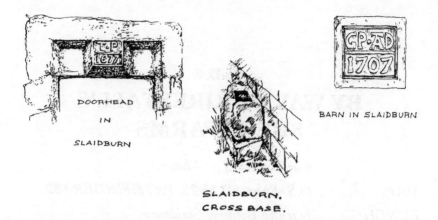

DOORHEAD IN SLAIDBURN

BARN IN SLAIDBURN

SLAIDBURN. CROSS BASE.

Past industries of the village have included hat manufacture, shoe and dress making and in the 19th century hand-loom weaving was carried out in the little community of Mount Pleasant at the top of the village.

Give the village a good tour of inspection before returning home, you will find that it holds many surprises to lovers of rural architecture. If this sounds too energetic after a day's walking, then just sit on the river bank and dangle your feet in the cool waters of the Hodder; one such tired walker only a few years ago found his feet resting upon a Romano-British large round quern stone; this is now on display in Clitheroe Castle Museum.

Hark to Bounty Inn

The 'Halmote' or Chief Court of Bowland was once held at Slaidburn (though occasionally in the old days at Waddington). The court room is still preserved and is located above the inn with access by way of the outside steps. Inside one can view the original oak furnishings of benches, dock and witness box, along with the open timber-work of the ceiling. Permission to view can be obtained from the innkeeper.

The name of the inn is a curions one and recalls an age when deer were hunted in these parts. The story goes that on one hunt day, a visiting squire, the Reverend Henry Wigglesworth, listening to the hounds giving voice outside recognised that of his own favourite hound; his exclamation of delight gave name to the inn.

Before 1875 it was simply known as The Dog Inn, and was one of the two

inns at Slaidburn, the other being The Black Bull. Since the 1930's the Bull has been used as a Youth Hostel, enabling many generations to appreciate Bowland's diverse countryside.

Slaidburn to Hammerton Hall

Take the road on the left at the War Memorial down to the bridge to pass over stile on right. Walk up the bank and cross the field on a right diagonal to corner of wall. Follow wall to trackway to pass over Holinhead Bridge and on up the track to Hammerton Hall.

Hammerton Hall

Hammerton Hall is a remarkable gabled and symmetrical Elizabethan Mansion of three storeys. The frontage presents a wonderful arrangement of mullioned windows; from ogee-stepped light to a transomed three-sided bay. The latter, sited above the porch doorway, was once used by the women of the house for spinning and tapestry work; the window affording much light during the day.

Hamerton

In the rear of the left wing is a spiral stone staircase and between the hall and the wing is a screens passage with two service doors. The present hall was built by Oliver Breres and it embodies the older house of the Hammertons.

The Hammertons were a powerful land-owning family, owners of Hellifield Peel and other large estates. Tradition holds that they could ride from Slaidburn to York on their own lands.

At the time of the Crusades Orme Hammerton gave two acres of land and the house at Edisford 'to God and St. Nicholas and the leprous brethren there

HAMMERTON HALL

for the health of my soul'. Edisford Hall at Edisford Bridge stands on the site of this hospital.

No Hammertons are now left in the Bowland district due to their involvement in the ill-fated Pilgrimage of Grace in 1536. It was through his part in that protest of the North against the dissolution of the lesser monasteries that Sir Stephen Hammerton was convicted of High Treason and executed at Tyburn.

Being a knight he was spared the ignominy of drawing and quartering and was instead hanged and beheaded. This harsh blow ruined the family fortune and sapped the will to live in his son Henry, who died in 1538. (See Walk 1, Volume 2 in the Brigantia series).

The origins of the Hammerton family are obscure, but it is possible that they were settled in the valley before the Norman Conquest. The first member of the family to gain some historical importance was Stephen, son of Richard de Hammerton, who witnessed some Pudsey deeds in c.1200, and who could afford to give the monks of Kirkstall Abbey twenty cartloads of hay per year. Stephen was a favoured name in the family and the memory of that name survives today in such place-names as Stephen Park and Stephen Moor.

Hammerton Hall to Lower High Field

Walk back down the lane to pass through the gateway on the left of the bridge. Follow the track up to Bell Sykes. Pass through the farmyard and follow the old lane up, following right-hand hedgerow around to enter Lower High Field via gate (notice the old cheese-press weight).

Bell Sykes and Lower High Field

Bell Sykes is an attractive old farmstead and still looks much the same as when it was built in the 18th century. Notice the old cobbled yard, made up of river-bed stones, a common feature around Slaidburn. In the rear garden stands a hand-driven grindstone, its sharpening days long over.

Lower High Field is a rebuilt 18th century house. A stone above the door lintel informs us that the work was carried out in 1876 for a person with the initials M.K.B. The lintel below is of a Yorkshire type with a date of 1702 and the initials W.W. & T.W. (Wigglesworth family?). Other remains of the older house can be seen incorporated into the fabric of the barn.

Overpopulation and congestion in the village of Slaidburn during the 16th century produced encroachment around a strip of waste called Highfield Green at the far end of the eastern common field or townfield. Slaidburn was the only township in the area with two townfields, the other being to the north west of the village. Today this encroachment is marked by the farms of Field Head, Higher and Lower High Field and Bell Sykes.

Lower High Field to Harrop Hall

Walk up to Higher High Field and on to a gate in the corner behind the lime kiln. Pass over the gate (there should be a stile here!) and follow left-hand hedgerow, over stile and into Field Head farmyard. Walk down the farm lane to the roadway. Follow the road opposite up, then left down and over the bridge (notice the old ford and trackway on the right of the bridge).

Walk on to pass over stile in hedge on right. Walk up the field on a left diagonal to go over fence-stile, and on down to go over wall-stile onto farm track. Walk on into Harrop Hall farmyard and around to the front of the house, permission from farmer having been obtained first.

Harrop Hall

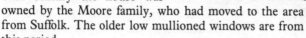

Hidden from view between Witton Hills and Easington Fell stands the lonely farmstead of Harrop Hall. The hall is partly 17th century and partly early 18th century. In the early 17th century the house was owned by the Moore family, who had moved to the area from Suffolk. The older low mullioned windows are from this period.

Above the main doorway is a Yorkshire lintel of 'key'
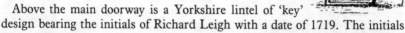
design bearing the initials of Richard Leigh with a date of 1719. The initials and date appear again on a stone above the barn door. The Harrison family live here today and life goes on in much the same way as it did 250 years ago.

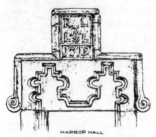

HARROP HALL

References to Harrop go back as far as 1274, when it was one of four wards in the Royal Forest of Bowland; these being Sclatbournewarde (Slaidburn), Baxholfwarde (Bashall), Chepynwarde (Chipping), and Harropwarde (Harrop). Each of these wards was divided into vaccaries (large cattle farms), one of these being Harrop Hall — Harrop Fold being the site of the hamlet.

The Fold lies on the east side of Harrop Fell and can be reached by a field track which runs past Harrop Lodge and Lane Ends down into the Fold. The main approach to Harrop Fold is by one of the few gated roads in Lancashire.

Harrop Hall to Easington Manor

Walk back down the farm lane to go over wall-stile on the bend. Follow the riverside pathway on the high ground above the stream to go over wall-stile and footbridge. Follow track on, through gate, and on into Cockshuts Park Farm. (To visit the earthwork cross the bridge and follow the track up to Skelshaw and on round to the barn. The earthwork is the mound in the field up on the left. Follow the track on down to go over the bridge and on to Easington Manor). Walk a few yards up the farm lane to go through gates on left at rear of buildings to follow riverside pathway to Easington Manor Earthworks (the humps and bumps).

Easington Bronze Age Circle SD 719504

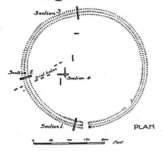

This oval earthwork, 182 ft. wide and 320 ft. long, crowns a small hill on the general slope of the east bank of Easington Beck. It consists of a ditch and bank with a gateway through the bank and a causeway across the ditch on the west side. Inside the bank and ditch the ground rises gently into a rounded hill, so that most of the inside of the earthwork is well above the level of the bank.

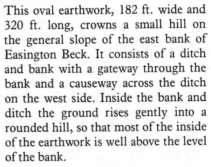

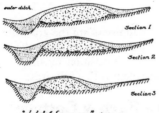

During the spring of 1934 a preliminary excavation of the site was undertaken by the late Dr. Arthur Raistrick. Three sections were cut through the ditch and bank and the inner area was briefly explored.

Although nothing was obtained to date the earthwork, the sections did show the ordered structure of the site and proved the presence of large floors that may well have been the site of huts.

The site could be compared with that at Fair Oak Farm, SD 648458, as both have a similar size and the same features are displayed.

Though a Bronze Age origin has been attached to the Easington monument, a later date should not be ruled out. The site has many features in common with the structures of the Celtic peoples of the pre- and post-Roman period.

The structure stands near Rye Clough at Skelshaw, both interesting names that warrant some investigation. Skelshaw is an Old Norse name which could be Skialdmarr's Wood. Or alternatively the Old Norse 'skiallar' meaning loud or resounding — being perhaps a reference to Skelshaw Brook, a rapidly descending stream nearby. Whatever the derivation the Scandinavian influence is apparent. Rye Clough suggests the type of crop cultivated on this once arable land.

Easington Manor

'Esintune' is another old Bowland village mentioned in the Domesday Book. This settlement never grew larger than two farmsteads. In 1284 the manor of Easington was held by Adam de Wannervill, one of the Lacy tenants in the Honor of Pontefract. In 1324, when Bowland was in the hands of the Crown after the rebellion of Thomas of Lancaster, another Adam paid half a mark for respite of homage at the Bowland Court Baron, but he never resided here.

In the 16th century the manor was held by the Bannisters of Altham, and one William Bannister built a house here in c.1552. This house was later extended by Richard Bannister in the late 17th century. Due to constant flooding of the site, due to its low lying nature, the house was abandoned some time around 1700 and the family moved to Newhouse in the higher division of Easington above Slaidburn.

All that remains of the former house of the Bannisters are the grassed-over remains of the collapsed dwelling — the humps and bumps. Over the years these have been the subject of an archaeological excavation by the Pendle Archaeological Group led by the County Archaeologist, Ben Edwards.

Easington Manor to Easington Barn & Cottage

Walk up into the farmyard and on to Easington Lane. Turn left and walk down to the barn (on the left) and roadside farm cottage.

EASINGTON BARN

Easington Barn & Cottage

Above the doorway of the barn is a framed date tablet of 169* with the initials R.B.A. (Richard & Alice Bannister) N.O.D. This datestone may have come from the old Easington Manor House or be, along with the barn, contemporary with it.

The delightful roadside cottage has a datestone above the doorway of 1699 with the initials H.E.S. To the rear of the house can be found a plain-style Yorkshire doorhead.

Easington to Newton

Walk along the lane to pass over gate *on right. Cross the field to far left-hand corner to pass through gates. Follow old trackway to river and on to Newton Bridge.*

Chapel Croft, Easington

In lower Easington, on the Waddington Road, stands a farmstead known as Chapel Croft. Although no evidence of a chapel standing on this spot exists, many locals talk of the existence of a burial ground and bases of buttresses on the land attached to the farm.

CHAPEL CROFT
EASINGTON

It is possible that the croft formed part of the endowment of a Hammerton Chapel at Slaidburn Church, though the evidence for this is not certain. The name 'Chapelcroft' existed before 1279 — in that year a certain Adam of Chapelcroft was murdered by Adam of Bouland, the latter being found guilty and hanged.

On the lintel over the house door the initials IPoIP and the date 1699 are carved. A datestone on the barn of 1671 bears the initials IP GP (Parker family). The remains of a 17th century mullioned window forms a bridge over a stream nearby.

A shorter return to Slaidburn via Dunnow Hall is now described.

Newton to Dunnow Hall

From Newton village walk down to Newton Bridge to pass through the small gate on the left to follow the riverside path to go over slab bridge and wall-stile. Follow wall/fence to the left to pass through small gate on left. Follow path on under the wooded limestone cliffs (this is a very good spot to find such fossils as Crinoids, Trilobites and Brachiopods) to pass through kissing-gate and on to the Dunnow trackway.

Dunnow Hall

Dunnow Hall was built in the 1830's by the Wilkinsons, ancestors of the present squire of Slaidburn, Mr. John Norgrave King-Wilkinson. The Hall stands on the site of a former 17th century house of Tempest Slinger.

Below Dunnow is a large area of land known as the Flatts. Early in the

19th century there was great poverty and distress in the Hodder Valley and relief work was organised, by which the Hodder (which till then flowed in a curve a quarter mile distant) was given a straight course down the centre of the Flatts.

In one or two of the fields are still to be found boundary or ditch stones to show, instead of hedges or walls, the divisions of the farmlands. Possibly these were more needed when the river flooded the Flatts which it does no longer, though in wet weather the pathway through Dunnow is often in a waterlogged state.

Dunnow to Slaidburn

Follow trackway to roadway and walk on to Slaidburn.

Newton to Gamble Hole

Walk up the farm track behind the telephone box to pass over wall-stile on side of barn. Walk up the field to go over gated stile. Cross the field to corner of wall and on through gate. Follow left-hand hedgerow up and round to go down to cross slab-bridge, then on up to go over wall-stile onto road. Go through concealed gateway opposite and cross the field on a left diagonal to pass through gateway. Follow hedgeside track to Gamble Hole Farm

Gamble Hole to Ellerbeck Hall

Follow farm track to roadway. Turn right, then left to follow farm track to Crawshaw Farm. Walk past the front of the farm to go through gate. Walk on, passing wood on the right to follow right-hand wall to pick up Pain Hill trackway. Follow trackway to farmyard to pass over wall-stile opposite. Follow right-hand fence down, over stiles, to go through gate at bottom. Follow stream down along the brow of the hill to go through gate and on down to Ellerbeck Hall.

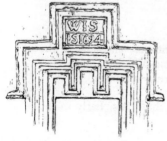

Ellerbeck Hall

Ellerbeck Hall, also known as Woodhouse Hall, is a large 17th century building. The Yorkshire lintel over the main doorway is dated 1694 with the initials W.I.S. & I.S. that belong to the Slinger family who lived here for many years.

In the 14th century the Abbot of Kirkstall had much land in the Bowland region. Woodhouse was then a stud for the Abbot's horses, the Cistercian grange of the Abbey being sited at Rushton on the upper Hodder.

During the 16th century encroachments took place in the Woodhouse area due to a population increase in the village of Slaidburn. The district became so populous that the manor records began to distinguish between the inhabitants of Woodhouse and those of Slaidburn village. By 1592 Woodhouse had grown into thirty-nine tenements compared with the mother settlement's forty-two.

Ellerbeck Hall to Cross of Brown & Myttons

Walk past the front of the hall to pass through the left side of the cow sheds. Walk up the field to go over a wall-stile. Follow left-hand wall to pass over wall-stile, following wall on to Myttons farm track. Walk up the track to the roadway. The base of the Cross of Brown stands by the corner of the road.

Cross of Brown

Along Woodhouse Lane by the former entrance to Myttons Farm is the stone pedestal of an ancient cross. Mossed over and ivy grown, this stone once held the old monastic cross known as the Cross of Brown.

Along the line of monastic roads, such as Woodhouse Lane, it was the custom to place 'crosses' at prominent points, partly to stand as landmarks pointing the way, and partly as a symbol of consecration or dedication to the service of the Abbey.

These crosses were usually in the form of a very plain stumpy shaft, roughly squared or sometimes bevelled to a rough octagon, and set in a socket cut in a large base rock or block.

Myttons Farm is now a Craft Centre specialising in hand painted pottery and well worth a visit as you pass by.

Cross of Brown to Slaidburn

Walk down to go through the yard of the Craft Centre and round to the front of the house (dated T.W. 1846. Another dated stone is built into one of the walls of the Craft Centre. It is a doorhead of Jacobean style W.W. 1872). A walled trackway leads to a field where you follow the left-hand wall to go through a gate in the corner. Walk down on a right diagonal to go over footbridge and wall-stile. Follow the path around Tenter Hill to go over stile. Follow streamside path to come out at the top of the village.

SLAIDBURN CHURCH

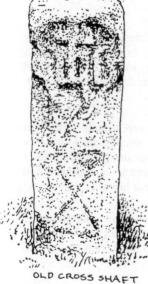

OLD CROSS SHAFT

St. Andrews Parish Church, Slaidburn

The church at Slaidburn, anciently known as the Wanden or Warden Chapel, is first meationed in c.1120 when Hugh de la Val granted the monks of Kirkstall Priory some interest in the 'Church at Slaydeburn'.

The tower is Early English in design, but has been subject to reconstruction many times. The massive angled buttresses were added when the west wall was rebuilt in the 14th century. Above the main west window are two highly Decorated image niches; sadly the figures have long gone.

On the south wall of the church is the Hammerton Chapel window belonging to the Decorated

period and the only one of that age in the building, the others being straight-headed with arched and cusped lights. The Hammertons had long associations with St. Andrews. In c.1250 Thomas de Hammerton was parson of the Warden Chapel.

Standing near to the tower is an oblong shaft with carved features on all four sides. It is known as the Old Churchyard Cross and once stood on top of the circular steps that are now the home of a sundial dated 1796. This stone was found by the late Rev. Lewes Jones, Rector, in the bank of the stream close to Dunnow Lodge. Upon one side of the shaft are the initials I H C (Christ the Saviour), on another an ornate letter M with a crown above (Our Lady), on a third side a shield bearing three X's. The fourth side is much worn and difficult to make out.

CROSS BASE WITH SUN DIAL OF 1796.

There are two 13th century tombstones, each decorated with a cross fleury. One is a fragment inside the church in the north wall and displays the sharp end of a hatchet or sword. The other is set in the outside east wall and shows a bow which curves upwards from steps, which is the symbol of a forester of the Forest.

Inside the body of the 15th century church
little has changed since the early 18th century.
There are many dated box pews (1616-1749)
and family pews standing before an impressive 17th century Chancel Screen that displays
much openwork finery. The Parclose Screens
are early 15th century work — very Gothic.

The three-decker pulpit is an attractive creation from the early Georgian period (1740).
In three tiers, it combines the parish clerk's
seat, a lectern and a pulpit. The service would
be conducted from the lectern and the sermon
preached from the pulpit. The clerk would lead

SLAIDBURN
CELTIC
HEAD

the responses from the lowest stall. These lofty pulpits became necessary
when high box-pews became fashionable.

The font is said to have once displayed Norman decoration before being
re-tooled in the 1840's. The font cover is Elizabethan, similar to one in Great
Mitton Church.

Built into the fabric of the north interior wall of the nave is a rather friendly
stone head. This is one of many Celtic stone heads that are found in the North
and points to a pagan origin for the site.

All the church doors have beam holes on either side, a reminder of the
lawless days when locals would seek refuge within the church walls.

Fragments of Mediaeval glass survive in the vestry window. These include
the figure of St. Wilfrid, recognisable by the seven-pointed star depicted on
his mantle, and the head of a monk in a white cowl (Kirkstall Abbey).

Slaidburn Church stands on the edge of a field known as Bad Grove — a
field-name which could denote an early settlement or sacred place.

In the field below the church can be seen a low raised mound. Upon excavation in the 1980's by the Pendle Archaeological Group beneath a layer of
riverbed cobbles was found over one hundred fragments of burnt bone, skull
fragments and some teeth. Flint and chert, along with what the Group described as a 'trial lead palstave' (axe) were also found. The evidence led the
County Archaeologist to ascribe a Bronze Age origin to the mound.

The Angel Stone

Today, an oddly carved stone stands in the chapel of Whalley Abbey Conference House. On first sight it would appear to be just another sculpted relic from the Abbey's ancient fabric. Yet nothing could be further from the truth.

The stone, known as the Angel or Slaidburn Stone, was found many years ago by the late Dr. Jackson of Slaidburn in a wall standing to the east of Slaidburn Rectory. For many years the stone stood in the doctor's garden, only to be lost when after the doctor's death the house was pulled down and rebuilt.

For decades the stone was thought to be lost, only a photograph gave testimony to its existence. From this photograph the late Prof. W.G. Collingwood was able to describe and date the stone. He placed a late 10th century origin on the stone and noted that there was a figure, 'the quaint angel', a coil and a swastika engraved in bold relief. These designs, he pointed out, had Norse origins.

The stone reappeared in a bequest to Whalley Abbey of Mrs Williams of Whiteholme, Slaidburn and now stands by the chapel window from where I have been able to examine it.

The figure could be that of St Michael the Archangel, but given the pointed boots and the odd position of the arms this cannot be so. I rather think that it depicts Volundr the Smith, with the artificial wings given him by the Swan Queen to escape his tormentors, holding his smithy tools (the story of Volundr can be found in the 'Lay of Volundr' in the collection of Norse poems known as 'Verse Edda'). The small cross with knobbed ends I take to be a swastika — mark of the Norse settlers. The coil or stopped plait is the Scandinavian Knot. The stone itself is only a fragment of a larger cross and other fragments may be built into walls in the village.

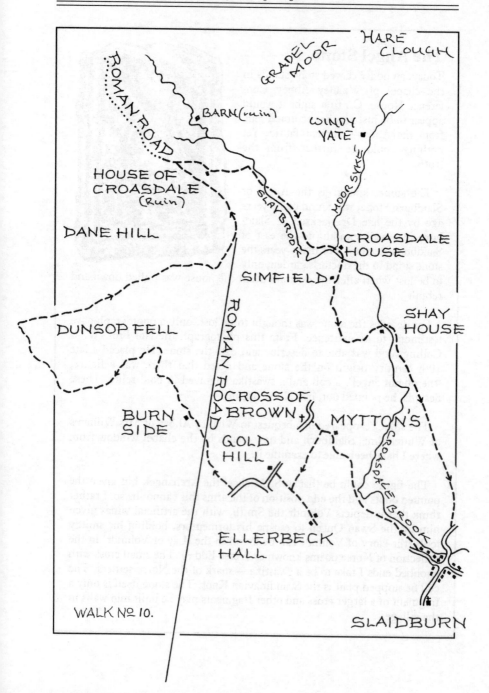

GRADEL MOOR

HARE CLOUGH

ROMAN ROAD

BARN (ruin)

WINDY YATE

MOOR SYKE

HOUSE OF CROASDALE (Ruin)

SLAYBROOK

CROASDALE HOUSE

DANE HILL

SIMFIELD

SHAY HOUSE

DUNSOP FELL

ROMAN ROAD

CROSS OF BROWN

MYTTON'S

CROASDALE BROOK

BURN SIDE

GOLD HILL

ELLERBECK HALL

WALK Nº 10.

SLAIDBURN

Walk 10

ABOVE THE LEGIONS HIGHWAY CROSSED

9 miles, 5 hours.

MAP: *O.S. SD 65/75 PATHFINDER 660*
LUNCH: *Packed lunch & flask.*
START: *Slaidburn.*

This walk gently climbs up the fellside to the vantage point of Dunsop Head where, showing through the ling and sparse grasses, the settlement sites of early man can be found. To the east Craven is laid out before us with the Pennine Aire Gap as a backdrop. To the north east the twin lions of Pen-y-Ghent and Ingleborough stand sentinel above the limestone reefs. As we descend to meet the Roman Road and the Old Salter Track we find ourselves in the rugged valley of Croasdale guarded by the granite fortresses of Reeves Edge and Bullstones. We leave this forlorn setting to return to the grassy knolls above Slaidburn and the friendly banks of the Hodder. This is a walk of great contrasts amid some very dramatic settings.

My thanks to E.M.B. Williams of Alcester for the useful remarks regarding the footpath between House of Croasdale & Croasdale House.

Slaidburn to Ellerbeck Hall

Walk up the road to follow the footpath sign 'To Woodhouse' after the Health Centre. Follow the streamside path through the wood to go over stile. Walk around Tenter Hill (a tenter field was a place where cloth was dried and stretched over tenter frames, being held in place by sharp hooked nails or tenter hooks in the early days of weaving) to go over wall-stile and slab bridge. Walk across the field to the far wall, pass through gateway and follow right-hand wall round to Myttons Craft Centre. Walk through the yard and up the lane to go left as the wall turns. Follow wall to go over wall-stile. Follow right-hand wall on over the hill to pass over wall-stile. Follow right-hand hedge to go over wall-stile. Walk down the field to pass through gates on the right of the cow sheds/barn onto roadway. Walk down to Ellerbeck Hall.

Ellerbeck Hall to House of Croasdale

Retrace your steps back to the last wall-stile and on to Gold Hill, following the road down, then to the right to enter Burn Side farm lane (or just walk up the road to enter the farm lane) and on up to the farm to pass over stiles to rear of farm. Follow track up to pass through gate. Follow the track on the right to go around and up the fell, keeping to the track that veers to the right as you near the top. Cross the mossy summit making your way gradually over to the wall on the left to reach the small gateway at Dunsop Head. Do not pass through the gate, instead walk directly away from it to the left of some scattered gritstones to follow the waymarked track down to the Salter Track/Roman Road. Follow the track up to the ruin of the House of Croasdale — off the track down on the right.

Crosdale or Croasdale

Croasdale is situated at the Slaidburn end of the old salter's trackway from Hornby. Travellers along this lonely fell-top road, as they pass through the wild and severe beauty of Croasdale Valley, may well marvel at the Roman engineers who paved a road across this difficult country. The line of the road is clearly traceable between Gamble Hole and Woodhouse and again over Bolton Head Fell making its way to Overborrow.

One of the earliest references to Croasdale is in the Kirkstall Cartulary; a translation of the Latin reads as follows: 'The bounds between Gradal and Crosdale begin at Wyndyhates, and so to the Slaybrok, and thence to Berkslacheyd, and so to the Bulstanis, and then to Crosdalheyd. Gradall from Crosdall to Hoder, and Crosdale goes as far as Wytlyngdall.'

The Kirkstall document suggests that the old name for Croasdale Brook was Slaybrook, from which Slaidburn takes its name — a sheep pasture; it also explains the origin of Whitendale, namely 'the dale of the white ling/heather. Berkslacheyd is Burn Slack above Burn House, and Bulstanis refers to the Bullstones on Croasdale Fell. Gradel, now practically forgotten as a place-name, was formerly the moor between Croasdale and Hareclough. The Wyndyhates was stated by the monks to lie at the beginning of the bounds between Gradel and Croasdale. The site of the Windy Yates (track/road ON) is now known as Clough and stands at the top of Moor Syke.

Little of architectural note is to be found at Croasdale. The House of Croasdale, formerly Hill House, is now in total ruin with only a small round-headed window surviving. Croasdale House was built in the 1640's, but little is to be seen from this period externally.

House of Croasdale to Simfield

Follow the path below the ruin to the stream and cross at bridge a quarter of a mile further down. Go up field and down to Croasdale House. Pass through the yard and on to go right to cross a gated footbridge. Walk up through the wood to go over stiles and on over next stile to the front of Simfield.

Simfield

This is one of the few buildings in Croasdale to bear an inscribed doorhead. Above the doorway of an outbuilding is a doorhead dated 1645 with the initials IB. EB. RB.,  along with the crudely carved initials HD. It is likely that the initials belong to the Blezard family, who were prominent in Croasdale before 1700.

Simfield to Slaidburn

Go over stile at front of house and cross the brow of the field to go over fence-stile. Walk over the hill to go over stile by gate. Left, and follow trackway down to go through gate and on through next two gates at Shey House (a farm is recorded here as early as 1367). Go over bridge and over wall-stile on right. Follow right-hand fence for 50 yards and on to cross the field to go over wall-stile by the gateway on the right. Follow right-hand fence to corner to cross the field to far corner to go over wall-stile. Walk directly up the field to go over wall-stile and on, over fence-stile, and on to go over next wall-stile. Cross the field directly to go over wall-stile in corner and follow wall/hedge onto road. Right, and walk on into Slaidburn.

CROASDALE

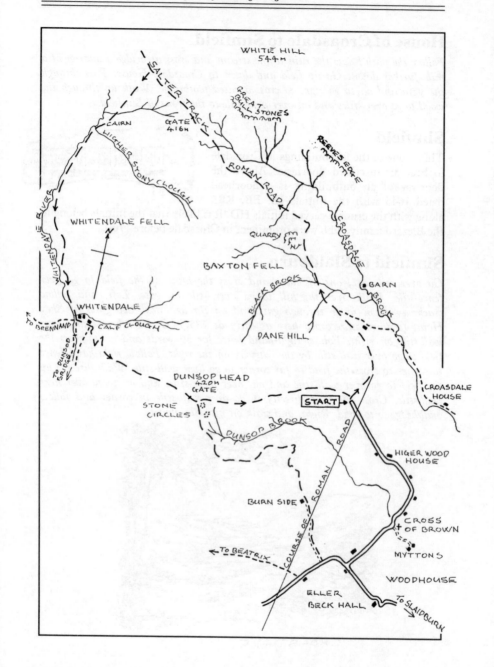

WALK No. 11

LONELY FELL WANDER

8 miles, 4 hours.

MAP: *O.S. SD 65/75 PATHFINDER 660.*

LUNCH: *Packed lunch & flask.*

START: *Top of Woodhouse Lane,*
some off road parking.

This is a good winter walk when the days are short and a fair stride out is needed without diversions apart from the views. I first did this walk in the early 1960s with my good friend John Mitchell on an early foray into the Wild Heart of Bolland. The remoteness of the place appeals to me now as it did then, one always wants to stay walking up here for ever.

Top of Wood House Lane to Whitendale

Pass through the gate and follow the trackway on, past the old quarry, to a gate at the highest point on the Hornby Road/Salter Track. Pass through the gate and follow the track on for some way to a minor high point near a number of large, spaced about stones. Here notice the waymarker post down on the left. Follow the track down passing cairn to river. Follow pathway down the river to join a track that leads to Whitendale Farm.

Whitendale to Dunsop Head Wall-Gate

Walk up through the farmyard to pass through gate onto rough hillside trackway. Follow the trackway as it zig-zags up the hill to follow waymarkers across the moor to the wall-gate at Dunsop Head.

Dunsop Head to top of Wood House Lane

After passing through the gate walk directly on, passing stone circle, to waymarker post. From here walk on veering to the right to join rutted hollow-way that leads you down to the gate at the top of Wood House Lane.

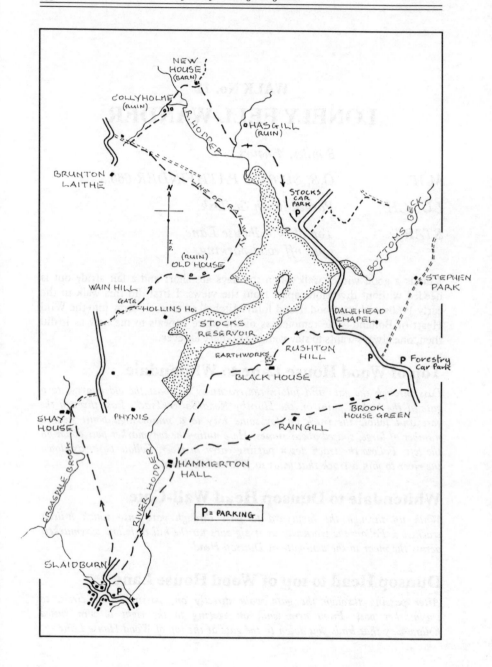

WALK No 12

CIRCUMNAVIGATION OF STOCKS

10½ miles, 6 hours.

MAP: *O.S. SD 65/75 PATHFINDER 660.*

LUNCH: *Hark to Bounty, Slaidburn.*

START: *Dalehead Chapel, Stocks Car Park or Forestry Car Park.*

The old village of Stocks at Dalehead was lost to the collected waters of the youthful Hodder in the 1920's, and only a few of the outlying farms which it served still survive — most are in ruin — such was Water Board policy then as it is now. Thankfully the reservoir is no longer out of bounds and some inroads for the public (the true owners) have been made. This is a very good walk allowing one to view every aspect of Stocks.

Stocks, Dalehead

The tiny hamlet of Dalehead, with its fine 17th century houses at Stocks and Rushton Grange, has now disappeared beneath that great expanse of water known as Stocks Reservoir. Major work on the construction of the reservoir began in 1922, but prior to this much preliminary work had already been completed. These works included the reconstruction of over five miles of roadway from Long Preston which could carry the heavy traffic to the depot railhead at Tosside, and the construction of a three foot gauge railway from Tosside to the site of the dam and quarries beyond, a distance of five miles.

A village to house 300-400 workmen and their families was built, along with offices, workshops and a cinema. The construction village is long gone, but in an old quarry near Cross of Greet Bridge, an old Rodley Smith steam crane remains to this day. The crane is mounted on a wheeled bogey that ran on a railed trackway. The engine has been removed, but the gearbox and boiler remain. The old church that stood at Dalehead was the only building to avoid a watery grave. It was taken down and rebuilt in 1938 further up the valley. It is a great pity some of the houses were not saved, but industry and commerce with their values based on short-term profit care little for the aesthetic character of past rural life. Some of the old dated doorheads from the village were saved and are now to be found in the yard at Phynis.

Natural History of Stocks

The natural habitats range from heather moorland, to dense coniferous woodland, small broadleaf woodlands and bracken-covered hillsides cut by moorland rivers and streams. The broadleaf woodlands are made up of hawthorn, rowan, birch and alder, the latter used locally in the manufacture of clog soles. Sitka spruce dominates the greater part of the forest area, though this generation is now being felled and a new mixture of trees introduced including broadleaf varieties along the side of trackways.

The heather moorland is the home of red grouse, whilst the forest attracts several species of titmouse, finches and occasionally crossbills. In summer the reservoir island is colonised by noisy breeding black-headed gulls who compete with local ducks and geese. In spring and autumn the reservoir attracts passage waders, and in winter a variety of wildfowl can be seen around the waters.

Dalehead Chapel to Hammerton Hall

Follow the farm trackway from the road corner to Black House farm, via cattle grid (notice earthworks in field). Pass rear of house to go through gateway on right into field. Follow edge of wood up to go through gate. Follow right-hand wall on to go over stile by gate. Follow track on to go over stile by gate and on, following right-hand fence to go through gateway into field. Walk directly on to go through gateway at the rear of Hammerton Hall. Pass through farm gate and follow farm lane on for a short distance to look over the wall on the right at the front of the Hall.

Forestry Car Park to Hammerton Hall

Walk along the road to turn right onto a farm trackway via gate. Follow the track on down, past Brook House Green (notice the stone slab-bridge in its rustic setting), into Rain Gill farmyard. Pass through gate and follow the well-defined track on to go through gateway and down to cross the stream by footbridge. Follow trackway up, through gate to follow left-hand fence around to Hammerton Hall.

Hammerton Hall to Slaidburn

Follow farm lane on, over Barn Gill (notice old bridge that was destroyed in a storm some years ago) and on to pass over Holmehead Hodder Bridge. Walk on a short way to leave the track to follow wall on left on to end corner. Walk on veering round to the right to go over wall-stile at Townend Bridge. Left and walk on into Slaidburn.

Slaidburn to Shey House

Follow road back to go over Townend Bridge and on to go over wall-stile on left (signed 'Croasdale'). Walk on and up over to the right to pass wall end and on following hedgerow and then wall to go over corner wall-stile. Follow wall on for 50 paces to veer over to the left to go over wall-stile. Cross field directly to go over fence-stile and on to go over wall-stile. Walk on and down the hill, following line of old hedgerow, to go over wall-stile. Follow left-hand wall to walk directly on over the field to far left-hand corner to go over wall-stile. Cross field and walk round to the left to go over wall-stile onto farm track.

Shey House to New House

Follow farm track up to the roadway. Left, and follow road on for some way to go over 'metal-ladder' wall-stile on right. Follow trackway on to gate. From here follow waymarked path over on the left on for some way to go over fence-stile by trees. Follow path on to cross wooded ravine via slate slab and on up and over to the ruin of Old House (on a fine day this makes for a good resting point with fine views over Stocks Reservoir and Gisburn Forest). Walk on to the right of the tree line to go down, past ruin of barn, to raised trackway (line of old narrow gauge railway).

Follow track to the left and on for quite some way to enter old quarry. Walk round the left-hand side of the quarry to go over fence-stile and on to gateway at trackway. Pass through gate and follow track on to hedgerow. Follow hedgerow down to the right to go over fence-stile. Follow the ravine down, over fence-stile and on down to ruin of Collyholme Farm. Walk down to the left to go through gate on right. Walk down the field to ford the river (usually easy, but during the wet months you may have to walk upstream to find a good crossing place — I usually wade across with the aid of two dustbin liners). Walk up the hill to go through gateway on right and on to the barn at New House.

New House to Stocks Visitors Car Park

From the east wall of the barn follow the trackway down to go over the river bridge and on to enter wood. Follow path through the wood to Stocks visitors car park.

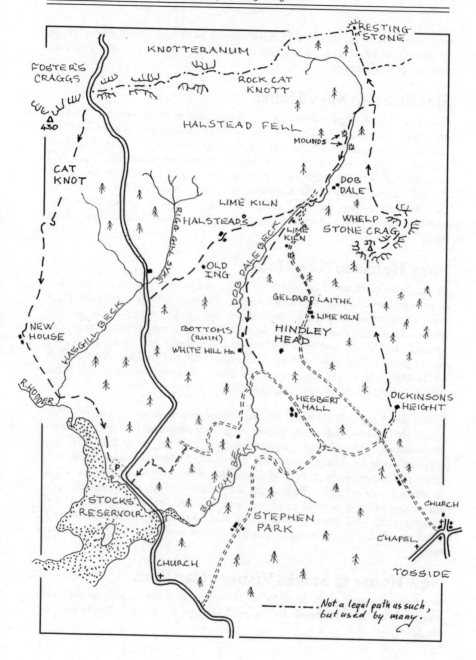

KNOTTERANUM

FOSTER'S CRAGGS

ROCK CAT KNOTT

△ 430

HALSTEAD FELL

CAT KNOT

MOUNDS

DOB DALE

LIME KILN

HALSTEADS

WHELP STONE CRAG

371 △

RIGG GILL SYKE

LIME KILN

OLD ING

DOB DALE BECK

GELDARD LAITHE

LIME KILN

HASGILL BECK

NEW HOUSE

BOTTOMS (RUIN)

HINDLEY HEAD

WHITE HILL Ho.

R. HODDER

HESBERT HALL

DICKINSONS HEIGHT

BOTTOMS BECK

CHURCH

STOCKS RESERVOIR

P

STEPHEN PARK

CHAPEL

CHURCH

TOSSIDE

—·—·—·— *Not a legal path as such, but used by many.*

RESTING STONE

Walk 13

GISBURN FOREST WANDER

14 miles, 6 hours + various shorter walks
ranging from 7 to 10 miles.

MAP: *O.S. SD 65/75 PATHFINDER 660.*

LUNCH: *Dog & Partridge, Tosside*
                   or packed lunch & flask.

START: *Tosside or Stocks Car Park.*

When walking in the forest area light no fires or stoves and be careful with cigarettes and matches. As always, keep your dog on a lead at all times.

Though full access to the Forest tracks and the crag tracks beyond is not covered by any agreement no one seems to mind so long as you keep to the pathways and do not obstruct the workings of those who live and work here. I have always sought permission before wandering at will, so stick to the paths I recommend and respect the rights of others.

Without a doubt the walks described here are some of the most rewarding in Bowland. I always remember coming out of the forest one winter's evening to view a red sun setting over the still waters of Stocks. The sky was red, shot with purples, greens, yellows and blues — a living Turner. On such a night the sense of freedom and a oneness with nature's beauty really comes home to you. I could have been in the wildlands of Northern Europe or in the depths of Canada, such is Bowland's best.

Tosside

Standing astride the Lancashire/North Yorkshire boundary can be found the hillside settlement of Tosside where Bowland's highest pulled pint may be had in that well favoured haunt of mine, the Dog and Partridge.

The pub, that started life as a Temperance Hotel, offers a good range of traditional ales and fine wines. Bar meals, using only the very best country

TOSSIDE

produce, with a daily changing menu are available lunchtimes and evenings except Mondays. From the Tap Room window the views over Gisburn Forest are superb. Well worth a visit.

The parish church of St. Bartholomew stands on the site of the old Hoghton Chapel and incorporates many of its 17th century features. In the sanctuary can be found a number of Jacobean pews of simple construction bearing the initials of local families.

The 17th century octagonal font is carved from Bowland stone and an inscription carved on five of its eight sides reads: 'Now that al children baptised heare God gave them good lives to lead the eternal God to feare 1619'. The simple Jacobean pulpit is dated 1701 with the initials of local families.

Mount Sion Chapel is a Congregational Chapel unchanged since it was built in 1812, with upstairs gallery. Known as Chapel House it has chapel and manse under one roof.

I shall describe the longer walk by way of the Resting Stone first, followed by the shorter sections through the Forest.

Tosside to Welp Stone Crag

Take the Forest road on the left of the Dog & Partridge and follow it on, past the saw mill to the junction. Take the right-hand farm accessway via stile and follow it up past Heath Farm (Dickinsons Height) via gates to walk on past Water Board pump-house via stiles.

Walk on, following left-hand fence to go through wide gap between plantations and out onto moor below Welp Stone Crag. Cross the moor and walk up to the Triangulation Point on the Crag.

Welp Stone Crag to top of Dob Dale

Walk on over the Crag to go through old gateway and on over to the left to go on down to the moor. Follow Forest boundary wall on to eventually enter trackway behind wall (fallen trees make this impossible for some way). Follow trackway on to end.

Top of Dob Dale to Resting Stone

Step over fence on left and pass through old gateway. Walk directly on over Gisburn Common up to the Resting Stone at top corner of Forest.

The Resting Stone

On the way up you will have noticed the birdwatcher's hide by the small moorland tarn. Listen for the bubbling calls of the curlews as they glide over their territories. On the lower ground you will find the 'tewits' or lapwings and in the highest places a sad, monosyllabic cry draws one's attention to the golden plover — 'the Pennine whistler'.

Five civil parish boundaries meet at the resting stone: Easington, Lawkland, Giggleswick, Rathmell and Gisburn Forest. It also marks the north east corner of Lancashire where it meets North Yorkshire, On our way to Foster's Craggs we will cross the boundaries of Austwick and Clapham cum Newby — see if you can pick out the marked boundary stones: E/L, E/L/A, & C/E.

Knotteranum? No, not a Latin word but an Old Norse one meaning 'a rocky hilltop/the knotts near a place called Raunum (Rathmell)'.

Resting Stone to Foster's Craggs

Follow Forest boundary over to the west, and keeping to the high land all the way the wall will lead you to the roadway by Foster's Craggs.

Foster's Craggs, Cat Knot

Below Foster's Craggs is a rise known as Cat Knot where a number of leaf-shaped flint arrowheads have been found. This may point to the Hodder Valley being part of an early trade over the mass of Bowland down into the Ribble Valley and central Lancashire in the Late Neolithic/Bronze Age times.

NEOLITHIC
LEAF-SHAPED
ARROWHEAD.

Over the many years that I have been wandering over the Bowland Fells I have noticed a great deal of evidence of early settlement sites: linear earthworks, circles of stone and circular enclosures being among the major sightings. A number of interesting sites have come to light where the peat blanket has eroded revealing the Neolithic floor.

Foster's Craggs to New House

Walk down the road to bear right at Cattle Grid sign to go through gate in wall. Follow the trackway on for some way (look back from time to time to gain changing views of the Craggs) to pass through gateway in wall. Follow path down to the right, then around to the left and on (we are now above the upper reaches of the Hodder Valley with the silent expanse of Stocks Reservoir before us), across a small stream and on down to pass through gate. Walk directly on to New House Barn (1814) in trees, via gate.

New House to Stocks Car Park

From the east wall of the old barn follow the trackway down to go over the river bridge and on to enter wood. Follow path through the wood to Stocks visitors car park.

Stocks Visitors Car Park to Dalehead Church

Follow the roadway on to the church.

Dalehead Church

This small church stands on a remote site as a memorial to the old community of Dalehead, when the village was submerged beneath the waters of Stocks Reservoir. It was built in 1938 from the stones of the old village church. The graves were removed and now lie in the present churchyard.

Dalehead Church to Stephen Park

Follow the road on to go up the Forest trackway on the left to Stephen Park.

Stephen Park

In an oasis of rural tranquillity amid a desert of pines stands the impressive farmstead of Stephen Park. The house was built in 1662 on the site of a hunting lodge belonging to the Hammertons of Hellifield Peel and Hammerton Hall.

The Park was established by Sir Stephen Hammerton, died 1501, who in order to build a park enclosed some 20 acres of arable land illegally, and dispossessed the inhabitants of their medieval vill of Hammerton associated with it. After the death of his grandson, another Sir Stephen, in 1536 (executed for his part in the Pilgrimage of Grace) the estate of Hammerton passed to the Crown. Stephen Park was then bought by Reginald Heber of West Marton.

Cheese Press, 17th century.

The main house is fronted by a single-storey gabled porch with a doorhead bearing the date 1700 with the initials I.H.A. (Heber of Marton). Inside the porch is another fine Yorkshire lintel with a wonderful design based on ornamental circles and scallops. A similar doorhead can be found on the rear of the house.

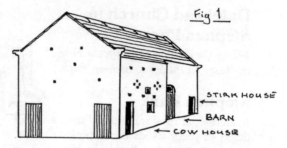

Fig 1

STIRK HOUSE
← BARN
← COW HOUSE

BARN AT STEPHEN PARK

Down the hallway we find a doorhead with a bold inscription: in relief: HE THAT DOTH PASE MUST HONEST BE NOT TO BOLD FORE YOU SEE. HMB. SE. 1662. The initials refer to the Molyneux (Mullineaux) family, inheritors of this Hammerton estate.

Whilst looking at the porch doorhead, notice the weight of an old cheese press by the corner wall, the base of which you are probably standing upon — it is an oblong stone with an incised circle and cross.

Opposite the house stands the Coach House, an interesting cart shed with two arched openings. Access to the upper floor is via an external stone stairway. To the rear of this building can be found an old latrine with a double wooden seat enabling folk to converse together before the advent of newspapers.

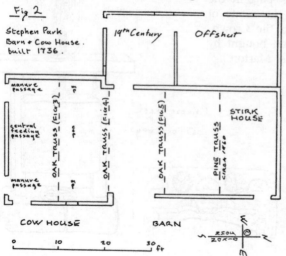

Fig 2

Stephen Park
Barn + Cow House.
built 1736.

manure passage

central feeding passage

OAK TRUSS (Fig 3)

OAK TRUSS (Fig 4)

19ᵗʰ Century

Offshut

OAK TRUSS (Fig 5)

PINE TRUSS CIRCA 1950

STIRK HOUSE

manure passage

COW HOUSE   BARN

0   10   20   30 ft

The barn to the west of the house has a datestone, 1736 with the initials J.H.F. (John Heber of Marton). This barn and cow house is a good example of early 18th century Northern rural vernacular architecture. Here we have a cow house with

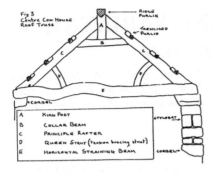

Fig 3
Centre Cow House
Roof Truss

RIDGE PURLIN
TRENCHED PURLIN

A KING POST
B COLLAR BEAM
C PRINCIPLE RAFTER
D QUEEN STRUT (tension bracing strut)
E HORIZONTAL STRAINING BEAM

CORBEL
STYLOBAT
CORBEL

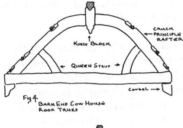

CRUCK PRINCIPLE RAFTER
KING BLOCK
QUEEN STRUT
CORBEL

Fig 4
Barn End Cow House
Roof Truss

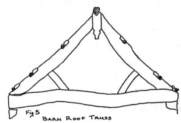

Fig 5
Barn Roof Truss

central longitudinal feeding passage and flanking manure passages added to the south end of the barn.

At the north end of the barn a stirk house is located. On the west wall of the barn is a winnowing door with a four-centred arched doorhead. Sadly the internal stall timberwork is missing.

The original roof trusses and purlins do however remain, and these are of great interest.

By the turn of the 18th century few large oaks suitable for building survived in Lancashire and Yorkshire. This economy of timber resulted in a gradual impoverishment of the roof truss but they still often preserved a pleasing form.

Such is the case with the collar beam and king post truss (Fig 3) at Stephen Park. Collar beam and queen strut trusses were in general use from the 18th century onwards.

The other two oak trusses make use of a king block (Figs 4 & 5) — a block of timber is set between the principle rafters at the apex of the roof, and this carries the ridge purlin.

The curved queen struts, positioned for tension bracing, are joined to a heavy horizontal straining beam giving support to the principle rafters.

Stephen Park to Tosside

Follow Forest roadway on and up to the left by the wood and over the rise to gain fine views over Dob Dale. Follow road on and round and up to a junction. Right, and follow road on to turn right down Bailey Lane, past the saw mill and on to Tosside.

SHORT WALKS AND VARIATIONS

Tosside to Halsteads via Dob Dale

Follow previous directions to the Top of Dob Dale, via Welp Stone Crag. Step over fence on left and make your way down to the stream. Follow the path that leads down Dob Dale Beck, past the two mounds and on down to the forest road bridge.

Dob Dale

Secreted away within the extensive forest of conifers can be found the Valley of the Dob. Here survive some of the ancient forest woodland, and a wide variety of trees can be observed on our walk through this arcadia.

Dob Dale is also home to a herd of Roe Deer that often emerge at night to feed on open ground. The Roe is smaller than other native deer and lives on its own or with small groups in conifer plantations, near water, feeding on leaves, berries and herbs. In winter the coat is grey-brown, changing in summer to red-brown. The antlers, rarely more than three points on each, are shed in early winter and regrown by spring. A sharp bark is its most frequent sound.

The two mounds we passed are thought by some to be ancient burial mounds, but I consider them to be glacial deposits. Saying this, just to the south of the mounds a burial urn was unearthed some years ago by forestry workmen. The urn is now in the Water Authority Offices at Dunsop Bridge.

Forest Road Bridge to Halsteads

From the bridge make your way down the right hand bank of the stream to pass over fence-stile. Cross the stream (notice old lime kiln on the opposite bank of Dob Dale Beck down on the left) and pass through break in wall. Walk up the hill to above the old limestone quarry and on and up over to the left to cross small stream by fence. Walk up the bank to pass over fence-stile.

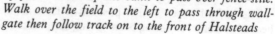

Walk over the field to the left to pass through wall-gate then follow track on to the front of Halsteads

Halsteads

The farmstead of Halsteads stands in the higher division of Easington below How Hill with extensive views over the Hodder Valley with the long back of Pendle in the distance.

The house, fronted by two large water troughs, is substantial with later additions to the original pile dominated by a beautifully proportioned gable. Upon visiting the house one is struck by its decorated cornice, unusually rich in ornament with a decorated string course. This is inscribed with the date 1687, with the initials of William Guy.

In 1556 John Guy bought Halstead from Ralph Greenacres along with other lands in Bolland. Then in 1592 'John and Richard Guy buy of William Guy gentleman, and Ann, his wife, six messuages with lands in Halstede'. It is worthy of note that one of the old bells, formerly in Slaidburn church tower, was inscribed the name of John Guy along with other churchwardens.

In 1644, just after the Battle of Marston Moor, the will of John Guy is proved, along with several other north country men who were wounded and died in the Civil War. The Guys are last recorded in the Slaidburn Register, when in 1644 Oliver, the son of William Guy, is buried; and in 1687, when William Guy and Alice Clarke are married.

Several architects have visited Halsteads over the years and have been struck by the decorated cornice window, wondering what such a fine example is doing here up on the wild Bowland moors. True, given the limestone underbed, Halstead has always been a most fertile piece of farmland, but the real wealth we observe here came not from farming but from money-lending: John Guy of Halstead's will of 1644 shows that he was the major money-lender in the Slaidburn and Craven district.

Halsteads to School Lane Roadway

Follow the farm lane down, passing the entrance to Old Ing — dated R.I. 1811 — and on down to the roadway above Coat Rakes Bridge.

Tosside — Geldard Laithe — Dob Dale — Hesbert Hall — Circular

Follow the Bailey Lane forest roadway, past the saw mill to upper junction. Continue directly on, passing the old quarries till you reach Geldard Laithe — a large barn on the right.

Geldard Laithe

Here we have a good example of an early 18th century barn, built on almost the same plan as that at Stephen Park: a cow house with central longitudinal feeding passage and flanking manure passages added to one end of the barn.

The shaped kneelers that form a termination at the eaves of the coping add a little grandure to the building.

The barn had a datestone, until it was wrongly removed, of 1702 with the initials G.H.E. HH.AD., thought to be those of the Holden family of Hesbert Hall. The importance of keeping datestones on their original sites cannot be overstressed; once removed and placed in another building they become an unrelated nonsense.

The Geldard Laithe datestone should be returned and whoever authorised its removal brought to book.

Follow the forest road on, passing a barn that is home to a Barn Owl, to go on down to the road bridge over Dob Dale Beck. Make your way down the left bank of the stream till you meet a fence. Follow the fence up and round and on down to go over fence-stile on right. Follow stream down to pass through field gate, then walk on and up to the left to go over fence-stile near edge of wood. Follow edge of wood on, over fence-stile and on to follow wall on to the low ruin of Bottoms. Follow forest wall on to enter trackway via gate. Follow track to go over stile and on to meet the Forest roadway.

The way down to the right crosses Dob Dale Beck and goes up to the left to follow forest roads and waymarked paths that lead one back to the car park by Stocks Reservoir.

The way to the left leads us past Hesbert Hall and on by way of the forest roads to Tosside or, if you wish, to Stephen Park.

Hesbert Hall

Many of the ancient farmsteads within Gisburn Forest are now in ruins; White Hill House, Dob Dale, Clough Hall and Bottoms are now only recognised by low foundation walls.

Hesbert Hall is a lone survivor within a green oasis amid the pines. Only a single farmstead remains today, but once several buildings stood: the remains of one stands as a low ruin with the remains of low mullioned windows still evident.

The datestone from this building, I.A.C.*I*T* 1673, was rescued by my good friend, the farmer at Hesbert Hall, Mr. Percy Tilbury, whose efforts have gone a great way towards preserving the architectural heritage of the few remaining farmsteads that once clustered around the ancient, now lost, village of Dalehead.

HESBERT HALL

Most of the old datestones and doorheads from the houses in the old settlement, such as Rushton Grange, have been saved and may one day be displayed in a lakeside display.

The ancient name of the farmstead is Hesebrithhaw, a name first recorded in a land grant made by John de Lacy in c.1235 to the monks of Kirkstall Abbey. Hesbert Hall then stood on the boundary of the de Lacy estate and that of William de Percy.

The Cross of Greet

The Cross of Greet stands above the Hodder watershed on the Slaidburn/High Bentham road at the boundary between Lancashire and North Yorkshire. Today only the base of the monument remains.

The stone is over five feet in length with a socket hole that took the former shaft.

CROSS OF GREET

Stones known as "crosses" have been used for many centuries as boundary markers and were first mentioned in the year 528. However, most of these stones would have come into use at a much later period, probably from Norman times onwards.

Boundary crosses were used by many landowners to mark out the limits of their land, often being referred to as "meare stones". They were used by the religious orders for the same purpose, and also used to mark parish boundaries, hundreds and shires. Some were simply pieces of stone without any decoration or particular shape. Others contained an incised cross on one or both sides.

The Cross of Greet, being a shire marker, was deemed important enough to stand in true cross form. Sadly, we have no record as to what the cross shaft looked like, except that on a map of 1598 of Lancashire it is shown as a stone supporting a cross.

In the 17th century the Cross of Greet was said to bound north east upon the lordship of Hornby. The Harringtons, Lords of Hornby, are believed to have had a boundary ditch on the hills between the Cross of Greet and the Trough of Bolland.

WALK No. 14

WALLOPER, WALLOPER WELL

9 miles, 4 to 5 hours.

MAP: *O.S. SD 64/74 & 65/75 PATHFINDER*

LUNCH: *The Longhouse, Harrop Fold.*

START: *By the cattle-grid atop Waddington Fell.*

On this walk we explore the most south-eastern corner of the Bowland Fells, an area of wild moorland that provides a home to many forms of wildlife. This is the Harrop section of Bowland, once one of four wards in the Royal Forest that were each divided into large cattle farms in the 13th century. With good views over the upper Hodder Valley, the Ribble Valley and over into Craven, this walk gives one the feel of being on the edge of Lancashire, a borderland of stone outliers.

Walloper Well

"The mason who built it, in love with a maid
Who brought him his dinner, one day, so 'tis said,
Was struggling to kiss her, when over the fell
A pedlar then passing cried, 'Wallop her well!'"

Not the sort of thing that would go down well in our age today, thankfully, yet it recalls a former age of rustic ignorance and has given name to a well-

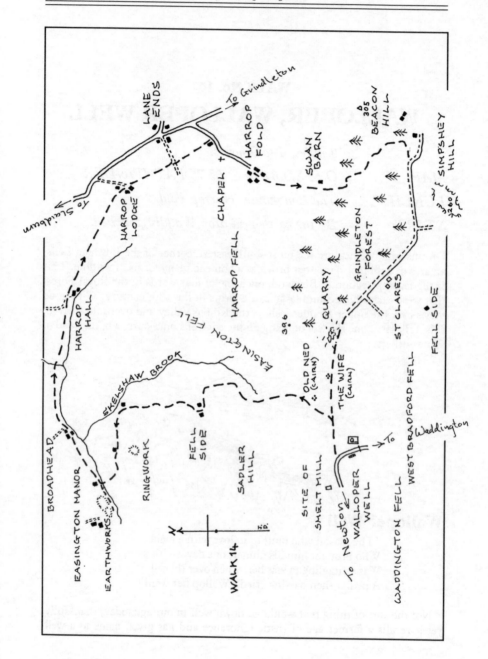

known Bolland landmark — a resting point on a journey over the fells. Spring water bubbles out of the rock to collect in three tiers of stone troughs flowing out of the last to wander down Smelt Mill Clough to join the Hodder via Foulscales Brook.

The feeling I get whenever visiting this part of Bowland is one of stepping back to a time before the Industrial Revolution. Here there are no torn landscapes — only a great natural beauty that filled me with awe when, as a young boy exploring this area with my friend John Mitchell, I first viewed this upper part of the Hodder Valley from the heights of Easington Fell.

Even now after years of discovering the area that evocative enchantment has never left me, throughout the seasons, and all they bring.

Walloper Well to Easington Manor

Follow trackway over the moor, left at fork and on down Skelshaw Brook Clough to enter Fell Side farm via gate. Pass through the farmyard and follow the farm lane down, past Skelshaw Farm and on down Rye Clough to go over Easington Brook low bridge onto the site of the Old Easington Manor House (the humps & bumps).

Easington Manor to Harrop Hall

Pass through iron gate upstream from low bridge and follow path upstream to enter Broadhead Farm via gate. Walk past shed and round to front of farmhouse via gates. Pass through gate and follow path on upstream, through two gates and on, following wall to pass over footbridge. Walk up to go over wall-stile on right. Walk on above the stream to go through gateway onto farm lane. Follow lane to Harrop Hall farm entrance (please ask permission to view front of house).

Harrop Hall to Harrop Fold

From farm entrance, follow wall up to the left to pass over wall-stile. Walk directly on over the moor to go over fence-stile and on to Harrop Lodge lane. Pass over old stone footbridge on the left of entry to farmyard and follow right-hand wall/hedge on, over fence and on to cross next fence near bed of stream. Walk on to pass through gateway onto farm lane. Right, and walk over bridge to pass through gate on left. Follow line of left-hand fence on to go over wall-stile on left. Follow wall on to go through gate on left of Harrop Gate Farm. Follow roadway to the right, past Harrop Chapel and on to Harrop Fold.

Harrop Fold

References to Harrop go back to 1274, when it was one of four wards in the Royal Forest of Bowland. Each of these wards was divided into vaccaries. It was at this time when the hamlet of Harrop Fold was established.

The main approach to the Fold is by way of one of the few gated roads that remain in the district.

An interesting feature to the Fold is its Chapel, standing in a field by the roadway, which has been in existence for 170 years.

Harrop Fold Farm is said to be one of the original Lancashire longhouses, today it is a highly recommended Guest House being a perfect hideaway retreat.

The drawing above shows the Manor House. Built in the 17th century it is the oldest house in the hamlet.

Above the Fold is Beacon Hill, site of an old fire beacon. These beacons were used to communicate some event or danger warning to those living thereabouts, and also act as prominent marks to guide the traveller.

Harrop Fold to St Clares

Pass through gate at the front of the Manor House (waymarked) and follow track on to go through gate on left. Follow right-hand wall on to pass through gate on right and on to Swan Barn. Pass through gate and walk up the hill on a left diagonal to pass through wall-opening and over fence-stile on edge of wood. Follow path up to the left and then follow old wall to the right, over fence-stile and on to go over next fence-stile.

Walk up to the left to fence-stile (do not go over). Walk up to the right and follow path through wood and then wallside path to stile in old gateway (do not go over). Follow path on the right, through the wood to pass through gate onto roadway. Follow road to the right for some way, through gate and up the road to the ruin of St Clares.

St Clares, Old Ned and The Wife

Sadly the farmstead of St Clares is today only a pile of rubble. I remember the ruin some years ago — its west wall was supported by three tall buttresses giving it a church-like appearance. The farm takes its name from a Dr. St. Clair who lived at Far House, Grindleton in the 1800s.

Old Ned and The Wife are two stone cairns, said by some to mark ancient burial mounds.

Greenwood and Bolton in their book 'Bolland Forest & The Hodder Valley' (1955) state: "There is also a rough stone circle on top of the fells above Easington, like the remains of an ancient fort and watchtower. To the east of these on Waddington Fell there is a most extraordinary assembly of tall bee-hive tumuli, built of rough stones, but so high and well-built that their purpose is hard to explain. Some day these may be explored".

St Clares to Walloper Well

Continue on up the track, through gate and on up to moor. Follow wallside track on the left, over old quarry and through old gateway. Follow right-hand track on to go over wall-stile and on, past The Wife (cairn over on right) and on to the roadway at Walloper Well.

THE OFFICIAL CENTRE OF BRITAIN

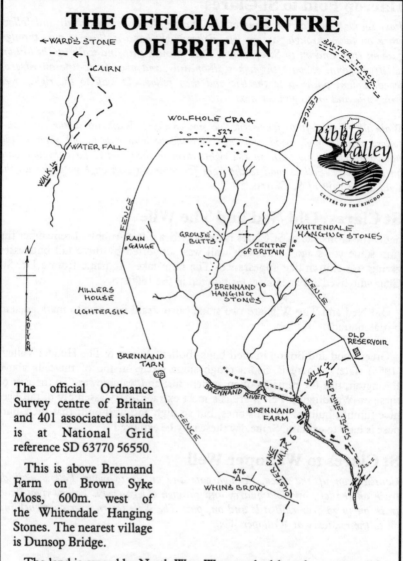

The official Ordnance Survey centre of Britain and 401 associated islands is at National Grid reference SD 63770 56550.

This is above Brennand Farm on Brown Syke Moss, 600m. west of the Whitendale Hanging Stones. The nearest village is Dunsop Bridge.

The land is owned by North West Water and, although not accessible to the public, walkers are permitted except during the grouse season.

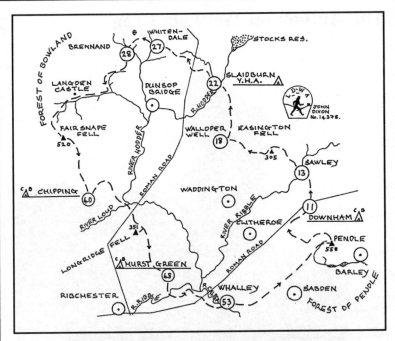

THE BOWLAND-PENDLE CHALLENGE TRAIL
85km — 53 miles

This Long Distance Trail that circumnavigates an Area of Outstanding Natural Beauty has been devised by John Dixon as a 24-hour challenge walk. It can be linked with the 47-mile Pendle Way to make a 'figure of eight' 100-mile two-day challenge. Alternatively, the Trail can be done over two or four days using YHA Camping Barns.

The Trail passes below the Whitendale Hanging Stones, above Dunsop Bridge, the official Ordnance Survey Centre of Britain.

For an illustrated guide, giving walking directions, gradient profile, details on Camping Barns and the Bowland-Pendle Challenge Certificate/Badge, send £3.75 to John Dixon, 8 Back Skipton Road, Barnoldswick, Lancashire BB8 5NE.

The Author on Wolfhole Crag